THE BEST
NEW
TEN-MINUTE
PLAYS,
2019'

T0352280

THE BEST NEW TEN-MINUTE PLAYS, 2019

Edited and with an Introduction by
Lawrence Harbison

With a Comprehensive List of
Ten-Minute Play Producers

APPLAUSE
THEATRE & CINEMA BOOKS
Guilford, Connecticut

Published by Applause Theatre & Cinema Books
An imprint of The Rowman & Littlefield Publishing Group, Inc.
4501 Forbes Boulevard, Suite 200, Lanham, Maryland 20706
www.rowman.com

Distributed by NATIONAL BOOK NETWORK

Library of Congress Cataloging-in-Publication Data
ISBN 978-1-4930-5317-9 (paperback)
ISBN 978-1-4930-5319-3 (e-book)

♾ The paper used in this publication meets the minimum requirements of American National Standard for Information Sciences—Permanence of Paper for Printed Library Materials, ANSI/NISO Z39.48-1992.

Printed in the United States of America

Contents

Introduction

In this volume, you will find thirty terrific new ten-minute plays which premiered during the 2018-2019 theatrical season, culled from the approximately 250 I read last year. They are written in a variety of styles. Some are realistic plays; some are not. Some are comic (laughs); some are dramatic (no laughs). The ten-minute play form lends itself well to experimentation in style. A playwright can have fun with a device which couldn't be sustained as well in a longer play. Several of these plays employ such a device.

In years past, playwrights who were just starting out wrote one-act plays of thirty to forty minutes in duration. One thinks of writers such as Eugene O'Neill, A. R. Gurney, Lanford Wilson, John Guare and several others. Now, new playwrights tend to work in the ten-minute play genre, largely because there are so many production opportunities. When I was Senior Editor for Samuel French, it occurred to me that there might be a market for these very short plays, which Actors Theatre of Louisville had been commissioning for several years for use by their Apprentice Company. I made a deal with Jon Jory and Michael Bigelow Dixon of ATL, who assisted me in compiling an anthology of these plays, which sold so well that Samuel French went on to publish several more anthologies of ten-minute plays from ATL. For the first time, ten-minute plays were now published and widely available, and they started getting produced. There are now many ten-minute play festivals every year, not only in the United States, but all over the world. I have included a comprehensive list of theatres which do ten-minute plays, which I hope playwrights will find useful.

What makes a good ten-minute play? Well, first and foremost I have to like it. Isn't that what we mean when we call a play, a film, or a novel "good?" We mean that it effectively portrays the world *as I see it*, written in a style which interests *me*. Beyond this, a good ten-minute play has to have the same elements that *any* good play must have: a strong conflict, interesting, well-drawn characters, and compelling subject matter. It also has to have a clear beginning, middle, and end. In other words, it's a full length play which runs about ten minutes. Some of the plays which are submitted to me each year are scenes, not complete plays; well-written scenes in many cases, but scenes nonetheless. They left me wanting more. I chose plays for this book which are complete in and of themselves, which I believe will excite those of you who produce ten-minute plays; because if a play isn't produced, it's the proverbial sound of a tree falling in the forest far away. On the title page of each play you will find information on whom to contact when you decide which plays you want to produce, in order to acquire performance rights.

This year, there are new plays by masters of the ten-minute play form whose work has appeared in previous volumes in this series, such as Don Nigro, C.S. Hanson, C.J. Ehrlich, Bruce Graham, Craig Pospisil, J. Thalia Cunningham, Jennifer O'Grady, Richard Dresser, and Nicole Pandolfo, but there are also many plays by wonderful playwrights who may be new to you, such as David MacGregor, Cary Pepper, Rita Anderson, Jeff Stolzer, Tira Palmquist. Laura Neill, Sharon E. Cooper, and David Nice.

I hope you enjoy these plays. I sure did!

AVALANCHE

by Rita Anderson

Original production by
Teatro Audaz San Antonio
Teatro Mundial: Love Makes the World Go Round—A Ten-Minute Playfest
May 25, 2018

Artistic Director, Laura Garza
The Cellar Theater
At Public Theater of San Antonio

Director, Holly Nañes

GINA, Lillie Gonzales
PHIL, Saul Valadez

CHARACTERS

GINA, lost, new to the city. Conservative, doesn't "cuss".
PHIL, a stranger at the bus stop, wears camouflage.

Age and race open.

SETTING

Downtown bus stop at night—suggested with a bench (stage cubes).

In camouflage (like someone on Duck Dynasty*), PHIL sits at a bus stop drinking from a paper bag, a ritual. He recites dirty rhymes.*

PHIL: "Beans! Beans! The magical fruit.
The more you eat, the more you—"

GINA: Avalanche! C'mere, kitty! KIITTTTYY! Avalanche!

>   *(Distracted, GINA enters with an i-pod on LOUD. She carries posters and tape. PHIL, safe in his vacuum, watches.)*

PHIL: Hey, hey, pretty lady. (*Beat.*) Nice rack!

GINA: You're a terrible person!

PHIL: Whah?

GINA: I can *hear* you, you know? You don't talk to women like that.

>   *(Removes ear buds.)*

You . . . JERK. Face! Big, dumb. Horse's . . . *neck*!

PHIL: Boo!

GINA:'Scuse me?!

PHIL: Your *comeback*? It's weak, but I'm glad to see you got a pulse.

GINA: So, now you're judging my *comebacks*?! Who do you think you are? Oooh, forget it!

>   *(She storms off.)*

PHIL (*ashamed.*) I'm sorry. I am. I. I say the wrong thing. A lot.

GINA: That's not good enough. What you said is *juv-e-nile*!!

PHIL: (*Nervous.*) "*Juvineelia*?" Am I gettin arrested? Is *that* some sorta penal code you gonna charge me with?

GINA: Good evening, Sir. You are obviously strange, and I'll avoid this block in the future.

>   *(Desperate for company, PHIL gets up to keep her from leaving.)*

PHIL: So ya' new here? Cause no one talks to me. They all think I'm *off*.

GINA (*nods.*) And there's a stretch!

PHIL Sure, sure. So (*Beat.*) why you still talkin to me?

GINA: Well, Mr. Downtown, you *know it all* so you tell me.

PHIL: Tell you what?

GINA: How new I am to the "big city!" (*Disgust.*) Full of trash and moral decay. A world in decline!

PHIL: I'd say brand-new cuz you look lost.

GINA: (*Lying.*) I am NOT "lost."

PHIL: I may be ignorant, Ma'am, but I ain't stupid. I watch TV! Or I used to. But now I do *this*!

GINA: What?! Harass women in the street?

PHIL: No, I people-watch. Who needs the canned stuff when I got the live feed right here with no commercials! And tonight? The channel's on *you*–and you're plenny worried 'bout sumthin.

GINA: You're not too good at guessing people then 'cause nothing could be more offbase! . . . And. And, the streets run numerical. On a grid. So, I am NOT lost!

(*She storms off in one direction. Then, she crosses the stage in the other.*)

PHIL: Don't get many single women out here nights, is all. Less they lookin' for comp'ny.

GINA: I am NOT single—and is that a "hooker" reference?? Really, so now I'm a prostitute?

PHIL: Just wish you'd lemme help you.

(*Beat as GINA weighs her options.*)

GINA: Ugh! Yeah, alright—but only because it's getting dark. (*Beat.*) You know these streets?

PHIL: "Do I *know* these streets?"!! Useda drive a taxi! . . . Hey! What're those papers you got?

GINA: Lost cat posters.

(She shows him poster. [They say, "AVALANCHE, LOST CAT" with a picture of a fat, white cat.])

PHIL: How did you lose your cat?

GINA: Look. We *did* just move in, so I don't know how—just that Avalanche is gone! Posters are probably just *another* waste of time, but what if Avalanche can't find her way back home?!

PHIL: A cat named Avalanche . . .

GINA: My husband named her.

PHIL: Uh-huh.

GINA: It's because she's all white.

PHIL: Sure, it is.

GINA: Like snow. Get it, an "avalanche!"

PHIL: Hey. You wanna beer? Calms the nerves.

GINA: Ugh, it's getting darker by the second. I should go.

PHIL: Hey, I'm Phil, and you are—?

GINA: Probably too late already!!

(She starts to exit so he stops her with a new tactic.)

PHIL: Sorry 'bout your cat and all, but as self-voted Neighborhood Watch Cap'n, I hope you're in as big a hurry to take them signs down after—*whatever it is that happens to animals that run off like this happens.* Oh, everyone's hot to hang posters, but no one ever returns to clean up the mess.

GINA: You really are a brute. Can't you see I'm distraught?

PHIL: *(Doesn't know the word..)* "Dis-traught"?

GINA: All the way off the map here. As in, Not In a Good Place!

PHIL: We still talkin 'bout the cat? Or is this some *other* avalanche?

GINA: *(Tense laugh.)* When I was scrubbing floors earlier, I heard a news story that was right up your alley, Phil. It said that *rude* people make more money. And you, sir, should be a millionaire!

PHIL: Look, I'll hep hang them posters—and two sets a hands will go quick 'specially when my pair knows where we're goin'!

GINA: And miss your bus?

PHIL: Oh, ain't no bus coming! City stops this route after five. Too much crime. . . . Now, you want hep with that "lost cat" or what?

GINA: Why do I feel like there's a catch?

PHIL: We'll get the posters hung and—I don't need your life story—just tell me *one* thing bout yourself.

GINA: I got nothing to say or to share. (*Beat.*) Okay, my name's Gina. Can we go now?!

PHIL: No, some fact that makes Gina Gina.

GINA: There's nothing special about me.

PHIL: Just any ol' thing.

GINA: Husband's in Afghanistan. (*to self.*) And he thinks *he's* in the war zone. Just look at this place! I have no friends or family here—but that's the life of a military wife. Always on the move!

(*She splits the stack of posters, hands PHIL half.*)

PHIL: How long's your husband deployed? When's he comin' home?

GINA: He isn't. (*Beat.*) Not now.

PHIL: Dear Lahd! I put my foot in it again? (*whispers*) Did he die over there?

GINA: (*Laughs.*) No . . . He's the one that's done the shooting!

PHIL: He kill someone? —I hunt, see, but don't know that I could pull the trigger on another man.

GINA: How about a woman?

PHIL: Whatcha mean? Is he in a co-ed corps overseas? No offense, but guys and gals bunking two-gether in lonesome country's just askin' for trouble. Wait, he didn't— You're not sayin'—?

GINA: No, I'm *not* saying.

(Zips her lip.)

Not another word. Can I have a beer now?

(He hands her a beer. They hang "AVALANCHE, LOST CAT" posters. GINA is about to exit down an alley {offstage}.)

PHIL: Oh, I'd skip that alley, Gina! That there's like a "latrine" fer the bums. And, you never did answer my question.

GINA: Did too.

PHIL: No. I asked for sumthin' bout *yourself,* and you told me about *him.*

GINA: Till today, all of me was pretty much all about him. Supporting whatever he was into.

PHIL: But there's gotta be sumthin'. About Gina.

GINA: *(Beat..)* I like to clean. I know that's dumb, but cleaning the house makes me *feel.*

PHIL: Feel what?

GINA: In control.

PHIL: Of what?

GINA: Of *something.* . . . Look. My husband left me, ok!! He just pulled up anchor and he . . . He *joined the other team*!

PHIL: He went AWOL?

GINA: Nope. He called, "SURPRISE!," to ask for a divorce.

PHIL: A divorce!! Is there someone else?

GINA: Ha!! Boy is there ever!

(Gulps down her beer.)

I got my "Dear Gina, I've left you for my <u>dear John</u>" call!

PHIL: *(taking it in.)* Oooh! Woah.

GINA: Yup!

PHIL: Soooo. Not a doe but a buck. . .

(GINA nods. Traffic sounds. GINA sits on the bench, depressed.)

Well. You. Bared your soul, Gina—and a pound of flesh calls for a pound of flesh. So, I gotta come clean bout sumthin.

GINA: Save it, Phil. I can't take any more "surprises" today.

PHIL: No, it's just. *(Beat.)* I wasn't no taxi driver.

GINA: No?

(Points at his camouflage.)

And, the hunting?

PHIL: I have never held a gun in my life.

GINA: Wow. Is no one who they claim to be anymore?

PHIL: Was a short-order cook, actually. Till my nerves went. Now, I live with my baby sister. She don't lemme drink in the house. So I come out here nights, to drown out the TV she sleeps in front of. I got nuthin, Gina. Nuthin. . . . But I make a killer bread pudding!

(They sit quietly, drinking.)

GINA: Husband said he couldn't live *one more day* buried in a lie. That he finally figured out who he was.

PHIL: And, now it's your turn, Gina!

GINA: I don't want a turn.

PHIL: I feel ya. But, your husband deserves to be happy, don't he?

(GINA takes off her wedding ring, throws it offstage.)

Gina, you see those two birds up on the wire there like black beads on a necklace? Know why they don't get scorched right offa them high wires?

GINA: Cause they're way up there! So high nothing can reach them.

PHIL: It's cuz they ain't grounded. Not touching ground or linked to it. So, the zap goes right through 'em and passes on.

GINA: Why did you tell me that?

PHIL: Cuz it's good to be reminded.

GINA: Of what?

PHIL: That zaps come, but they also gonna go. Gotta let 'em pass, right on through you sometimes.

(Beat. After the moment sinks in, PHIL stands and points with the posters.)

Wanna hang these last ones? Bars'll be jumping soon. Maybe someone's seen your, your Avalanche.

GINA: Okay, Phil. Yeah. . . . But, can I just hang here a minute?

PHIL: Course, Gina! Course. Be my guest.

GINA: I . . . I just can't face the emptiness of home yet.

(PHIL settles back onto the bench next to her.)

PHIL: You stay, Gina. Just stay and be a—a bird on my wire, as long as you like.

(They toast.)

BETWEEN HERE AND DEAD

by Merridith Allen

Original production by
Ruddy Productions
May 22, May 29, and June 5, 2018

Director, Joshua Warr

MICHAEL, Kirk Koczanowski
CAROL, Flora McGill

CHARACTERS

MICHAEL, Carol's boyfriend.
CAROL, 20s, Michael's girlfriend.

TIME

The present.

SETTING

An apartment in Washington Heights.

Lights rise, on Michael and Carol's kitchen, in a run-down Washington Heights apartment.

MICHAEL: . . . no, no, what I'm saying is, if I'm not around, and you need a dick, then it's OK. You can't fall for the guy, though. Separate that shit. Mentally. (*Pause.*) Also, emotionally.

(*He attempts to hold her.*)

CAROL: You touch me right now, I'm gonna slap you.

MICHAEL: Honey, you think I like the idea of some other man in my house—in my bed—?

CAROL: I dunno, do you?

MICHAEL: —this is me, takin' care of you—hey, hey, no. The answer is no, of course I don't like it.

CAROL: So why are you—

MICHAEL: —I'm trying to be sensitive to—

CAROL: —pushing on me to go find some other guy—

MICHAEL: —what you need and—

CAROL: —I need a time machine, right in this moment. How 'bout that? So I can hand it over to you, and say, hey, Michael! Maybe you wanna step inside this thing, go back, what, twenty to twenty-five years, so you never meet that asshole, Charlie—

MICHAEL: I never met Charlie, I never would've met you.

CAROL: Wha—we were all around the neighborhood—

MICHAEL: Yeah, but you hadn't dated my best friend for all of .5 seconds—

CAROL: Dated is an extremely strong word for what that was.

MICHAEL: Still. He brought you down to the club, you were wearing that little red number of yours . . .

(*He takes her hand, spins her to him.*)

CAROL: Stop it, right now.

MICHAEL: . . . baby, you about gave me a heart attack, swingin' these hips—

CAROL: I told you, stop . . .

MICHAEL: You don't want that.

(She doesn't, but she breaks away, anyway.)

CAROL How long, you think?

MICHAEL: I don't know.

CAROL: Ballpark.

MICHAEL: Tops . . . maybe five years.

CAROL: Fuck.

MICHAEL: Minimally, year and a half. Give or take. (*Pause.*) Charlie though, he's . . . going to die in prison.

CAROL: Why did you do it?

MICHAEL: I . . . had to.

CAROL: My mother told me, you know, she said you were trouble. The both of you.

MICHAEL: Yeah, but you like a little trouble, don't you?

(He tries kissing on her.)

CAROL: Who you want me to be fucking, huh, Michael? You got someone in mind?

MICHAEL: Shit. No. I don't wanna hear about it. Just—I don't want you to be lonely or—look, you know I know what a freak you are—

CAROL: Cut it out—

MICHAEL: —you can't go a day without—

CAROL: I said—

MICHAEL: We're adults here. Might as well just lay the cards out. You know what you need. I know what you need.

CAROL: How 'bout I'm lookin' at what I need—*who* I need, right now?

(Pause.)

MICHAEL: You gonna come visit me?

CAROL: No.

MICHAEL: Really?

CAROL: You gonna have problems in there?

MICHAEL: What kind of problems?

CAROL: You know what kind.

MICHAEL: I'm not gonna fall off the wagon—

CAROL: Yeah, I think you will.

MICHAEL: I won't.

CAROL: Five years, Mike? You think you won't?

MICHAEL: Could be a year and a half. Maybe less.

CAROL: Time is time.

(*Pause.*)

MICHAEL: You want a promise or something?

CAROL: I think I wanna break this off.

MICHAEL: Carol, don't say that—

CAROL: I don't wanna say it, believe me.

MICHAEL: You're the only reason I'm gonna make it. Thinking about you—

CAROL: Maybe you should've done some different things in your life. Made some different decisions.

MICHAEL: Don't do this—

CAROL: I have to—

MICHAEL: DO NOT DO THIS, CAROL! (*Pause.*) Charlie saved me, honey. I was—I owed this guy, I didn't have the money, he put a gun to my head. Right here. Like this.

CAROL: I can't—

MICHAEL: LOOK AT ME! PLEASE!

(*She does.*)

You know what happens when you're starin' down the barrel of a gun like that? You know what you think about? All the shit you never did or said that could've made a difference—that could've led you down another path. I was thinkin' about you. About your red dress and Charlie with his arm around you and how I thought I was lookin' at my future wife, despite that Charlie is my boy.

I was thinkin' about the time my mom didn't come home that one night from the crack house and how me and Charlie went to get 'er. I was thinkin' about that, one day I wanna see little kids runnin' around with my cheeks and your eyes and both of our stubborn personalities—I saw a million things, in like, the whisper of a second. Talk about a time machine . . . the split second between here and dead, that's a time machine . . .

Next thing I knew, ear-splitting shot, and this dude's face goes slack. He crumples, hits the floor like a puppet when you cut the strings off. Then I see Charlie, a .45 in his hands, shaking.

That's the truth . . . Charlie killed a man, cause it was that guy or me. That's why—the real reason why—I had to help 'im. I had to try to make it right for him too—had to get that body outta there, but—

CAROL: God . . .

MICHAEL: Yeah . . . what can I tell you . . . I fucked up. I always fuck everything up.

CAROL: Why did you owe him? (*Pause.*) Why did you owe that guy money you couldn't pay him back?

MICHAEL: I wanted to get us out of here. These roach infested walls. I saw . . . what I thought was an opportunity, investment-wise. I didn't tell you, cause I wanted to surprise you, you know? . . . I thought I had it this time. A way out.

CAROL: Nobody makes it out like that. Those type of people.

MICHAEL: I know that . . . I think I always knew that. I still had to try. (*Pause.*) You really won't visit me?

(*She moves to him, scoops him into her arms.*)

CAROL: I'll visit you.

(*Long pause.*)

I'll visit you.

THE BIG SHELL
A MATH NOIR

by Craig Pospisil

Presented by
The NOW Collective
Barrow Group Studio Theatre
New York
July 29, 2017

Director, Sean T. McGrath

PHILIP FIBONACCI, Raul Hernandez
BROOKE TAYLOR / CIGARETTE GIRL, Samantha Evans
EMMY, McKenna DuBose
DARK FIGURE / HOBSON, Sean T. McGrath
GUNSEL, Therese Dizon
PAUL GUTTMANN, Morgan Bartholick

CHARACTERS

PHILIP FIBONACCI, a private detective.
BROOKE TAYLOR, a damsel in distress. Or is she?
EMMY, Fibonacci's loyal secretary.
DARK FIGURE, not long for this world.

CIGARETTE GIRL, a leggy young woman selling tobacco from a tray (can be played by the actress playing BROOKE).

PAUL GUTTMANN, a very rotund owner of an illegal casino.

GUNSEL, Guttmann's bodyguard, a gunsel.

HOBSON, a police detective (can be played by the same actor as DARK FIGURE).

SETTING

San Francisco, all in shadows and black and white.

TIME

The 1940s. Of course.

It's a cold, foggy night in late 1946 down by the docks in San Francisco. PHILIP FIBONACCI enters and stands at the edge of a pier. He wears a tan overcoat, tied at his waist with a belt, and a fedora. He looks a lot like someone trying to look like Humphrey Bogart. He speaks to the audience.

FIBONACCI: It was cold and wet and after midnight, and the old piers on the San Francisco Bay was the last place I wanted to be. But I was on a case. And if you want answers, sometimes a case will take you places you don't want to go.

(Part of the stage becomes his office. FIBONACCI crosses and sits in a chair, with his feet up on the desk.)

It all started one minute after two on a grey November afternoon, when the clouds hung over San Francisco the way an exponent hangs over the base number. I was resting my eyes, when three raps on my door woke me from a dream brought on by drinking a fifth of whiskey.

(Three taps on the door to his office are heard, and a beautiful woman, BROOKE TAYLOR, enters, wearing a smart jacket and skirt suit and bright red lipstick.)

I'd never been good at math, but I knew something about figures. And this one had curves that'd make Euclid weep.

(EMMY, FIBONACCI's secretary steps in.)

EMMY: I'm sorry, Phil. She just barged in before I could stop her.

FIBONACCI: That's okay, Emmy. I'll see what she wants.

(Reluctantly, EMMY exits.)

BROOKE: Are you Mr. Fibonacci?

FIBONACCI: That's what it says on the door.

BROOKE: Actually, it says Fibonacci and Lucas.

FIBONACCI: Lucas got rubbed out.

BROOKE: He was killed?

FIBONACCI: No, he retired and moved to Fresno. I mean, I rubbed his name off the door.

BROOKE: But it's still legible.

FIBONACCI: Look, I'm a private dick, not a window washer. Why don't you tell me why you're here, Miss . . . ?

BROOKE: Taylor. Brooke Taylor. I've been robbed. I've been robbed, and I need you to help recover a golden nautilus.

FIBONACCI: A nautilus? That's a kind of seashell, right? Why come to me? The cops are pretty good at this sort of thing, and they don't charge eight dollars an hour, plus expenses.

BROOKE: It's . . . I'd like to keep this matter quiet.

FIBONACCI: Quiet is my middle name. So, what's this jam you're in?

BROOKE: I . . . Yes, all right. Somehow I feel I can trust you. The thing is . . . I'm being blackmailed.

FIBONACCI: Who by?

BROOKE: That's just it, I don't know.

FIBONACCI: What've they got on you?

BROOKE: Have you heard of a man named Paul Guttmann?

FIBONACCI: Sure. He runs an underground casino in Sausalito with tables for craps and roulette. What happened? You place too many bets on black thirteen?

BROOKE: Twenty-one is my game.

FIBONACCI: Cards, huh? Okay, so how much do you owe?

BROOKE: Thirty-four.

FIBONACCI: Grand?

(He lets out a whistle.)

That is one whole number. So where does this shell fit in?

BROOKE: I've been saving money to pay off Guttmann, and hiding it in the nautilus. I had almost all of it. But last night someone ransacked my home and took the nautilus. I just have to get it back. It's priceless.

FIBONACCI: Well, pardon me for asking, but if this golden shell's worth so much, why didn't you sell it to pay your bills?

BROOKE: It belongs to my father. It was a gift from President Roosevelt. A medal of sorts. My father invented a secret code the Navy used during the war that the Japanese could never break. My father would be humiliated if my gambling debts were known.
    Can you help? I'm afraid I don't have much money.

FIBONACCI: I don't know, sister. I've got bills too. I need to get someone to clean Lucas' name off the door for one thing.

BROOKE: If you'd help me, I . . . I'd do anything.

FIBONACCI: Anything?

BROOKE: Yes, but . . . Oh, you don't mean . . . ? You wouldn't.

FIBONACCI: I might. It's been fifty-five days. Not that I'm counting.

(BROOKE dissolves into tears.)

FIBONACCI: (*To the audience.*) She turned on the waterworks. They worked.

(To BROOKE.)

All right, so how'd they contact you?

BROOKE: This note arrived this morning.

(She hands him a folded piece of paper.)

FIBONACCI: "I know what's going on with you and Guttmann. Meet me at Pier 89 at 1:44 a.m. I want my cut or everything will be on the front page of the *Chronicle*."

(He turns over the note, looking for more.)

Is this all of it?

BROOKE: That's all there was.

FIBONACCI: What's he mean by his "cut?"

BROOKE: I don't know. That's why I'm so scared. What do I do?

FIBONACCI: Go home for now. I'll check into things and call you later.

BROOKE: Thank you.

(She turns to go, then stops, kisses him on the cheek, and exits. He sits and looks at the paper in his hand. EMMY walks in, sits on the edge of his desk and wipes the lipstick off his cheek.)

EMMY: I see you took the case.

FIBONACCI: Some case. There's about 233 things wrong with it already.

EMMY: Don't you believe her?

FIBONACCI: She's my client. I'm not paid to believe her.

EMMY: And did she pay you?

FIBONACCI: She'll pay me when it's over.

EMMY: That's what you said about the last one. $377 you got stiffed.

FIBONACCI: Listen, angel, I don't need—

EMMY: Why do you always fall for the troubled girls, when there's nice ones around just waiting for their chance?

FIBONACCI: Oh, really? And just where—

(There is a loud bang or thump from the outer office. FIBONACCI and EMMY jump to their feet. A DARK FIGURE in a black overcoat stumbles into the office and then collapses on the floor. An object wrapped in newspapers rolls from the figure's grasp.)

Who are you? What's this about? Say something.

DARK FIGURE: Sssi . . . Sssssix . . six-ten.

EMMY: What's he saying?

DARK FIGURE: Nuh . . . nuh . . .

FIBONACCI: Come on, spit it out.

DARK FIGURE: Nine . . . eighty-seven.

FIBONACCI: What's this with the numbers?! What's it add up to?

(The DARK FIGURE goes limp.)

EMMY: He's dead!

(FIBONACCI picks up the object wrapped in newspaper and presses it into EMMY's hands.)

FIBONACCI: Emmy, I want you to go to your mother's. Take this item with you. Sit tight. Don't answer the door. I'll call you later. What's your mother's number?

EMMY: Klondike-1597. Be careful, Phil.

FIBONACCI: Always. Now go.

(EMMY takes the package and leaves. FIBONACCI searches the body, but finds nothing. He's about to give up, when he notices something about the hands.)

FIBONACCI: There was no ID on the body, but I did find a clue. One hat confirmed my next stop.

(Another part of the stage becomes GUTTMAN's casino. GUTTMAN enters and looks out over his guests. He is a large man in a suit [think Sidney Greenstreet]. A CIGARETTE GIRL enters, with a tray of cigars and cigarettes. FIBONACCI crosses to the casino area from his side of the stage.)

CIGARETTE GIRL: Cigars, cigarettes. Cigars, cigarettes. Cigars . . .

(She sees FIBONACCI.)

Oh. Well, good evening, sir. Welcome to Guttman's Casino. See anything you like?

FIBONACCI: What if I say yes?

CIGARETTE GIRL: Then I might say yes.

FIBONACCI: Those are good odds. But I can't roll those dice right now. I'm here to see the fat man.

CIGARETTE GIRL: Your loss.

(The CIGARETTE GIRL exits, and FIBONACCI approaches GUTTMANN, but as he gets closer a bodyguard, a GUNSEL, enters and steps between them. The GUNSEL is slight and young, but very intense and he or she glowers at FIBONACCI.)

GUNSEL: Where do you think you're going?

FIBONACCI: I came to speak to Mr. Guttmann.

GUNSEL: Suppose he doesn't want to talk to you?

FIBONACCI: Suppose it's the converse.

GUNSEL: Oh, college boy, huh?

FIBONACCI: Is that your hypothesis?

GUNSEL: Suppose I march you out of here, college boy?

FIBONACCI: Then we'd be diametrically opposed.

(GUTTMANN finally turns to face FIBONACCI having heard this exchange.)

GUTTMAN: Please, please, let's not degenerate into fisticuffs, shall we? That would rather upset my guests. You must forgive Max here. He is employed to protect my person, and his devotion to that position is in direct proportion to my size, I'm afraid. Now, you sir, if you'll pardon my saying so, you look like a man who knows how to handle himself. And when a man who knows how to handle himself comes into my establishment, well, quite frequently we find ourselves at odds. No doubt you have no wish to be fractious, but one must to be cautious, don't you agree? Guttmann is my moniker, sir. And you are?

FIBONACCI *(To the audience.)* I didn't know what a moniker was, but I didn't want to ask and look stupid, so I played along.

(To GUTTMANN.) My name's Fibonacci.

GUTTMANN: Splendid, splendid. Now, sir, what is your pleasure? We have games of chance, we have spirits, or perhaps you desire some companionship . . . ?

FIBONACCI: I'm here about a nautilus.

(There is a pregnant pause. GUTTMANN's face is a stern mask, then he breaks into a smile.)

GUTTMANN: Really, sir, you are quite extraordinary. There's no other word for it. Well, I like a man who's plain spoken and who speaks plainly, yes, I do. What would you say if I said I don't know anything about a nautilus?

FIBONACCI: Then I'd say you were a liar.

GUNSEL: Why you—!

(The GUNSEL takes a step toward FIBONACCI, but GUTTMANN holds out a hand and stops him.)

GUTTMANN: There, there, Max. Yes, sir. A plainspoken man. I could use a man like you, sir. Yes, I could. Let me speak plainly with you as well then. Miss Taylor is not to be trusted.

FIBONACCI: I'm not sure what you're talking about.

GUTTMANN: Don't be obtuse, sir. You know precisely what I mean. Miss Taylor has not given you all the conditions of this particular problem. Nor has she been honest about its true value.

FIBONACCI: Do you mean the nautilus?

GUTTMANN: I do indeed, sir.

FIBONACCI: She said she bought it in Chinatown for $25.84.

GUTTMANN: How droll. Really, sir, I do believe you're pulling my leg.

FIBONACCI: Yeah, all right, you got me there. Actually, she told me it was a medal her father got from Roosevelt.

GUTTMANN: True enough. But there is a corollary. A parallel meaning, as it were, to the shell. The key to her father's cypher is derived from the golden ratio of the shell itself. To certain foreign powers, shall we say, that nautilus is worth an amount that is exponentially more than its weight in gold.

FIBONACCI: So, you're a Red?

GUNSEL: Keep pushin' it, pal.

GUTTMANN: Please, Max, please. Let us not take offense at labels. Left and right are merely diverging lines on a graph, sir. I am a business man. A business man looking to make a business proposition to a man who is interested in a business proposition. Are you such a man?

FIBONACCI: I haven't called the cops on you yet.

GUNSEL: I'd like to see you try.

GUTTMAN: Max, please. Don't be irrational.

FIBONACCI: Yeah, Maxie, why so negative?

GUTTMANN: That's enough, sir. Let us not take this tangent. Do you have the nautilus?

FIBONACCI: No, but I know where it is.

GUTTMANN: Excellent. Can we agree on a figure then?

FIBONACCI: I certainly hope so. How's forty-one eighty-one?

GUTTMAN: That's an odd number.

FIBONACCI: Maybe we can round it up. How 'bout you meet me tonight. On the pier. I'm betting you got a note about that too.

GUTTMANN: By gad, you are a clever man, sir. How did you know?

FIBONACCI: The law of averages. I bet you're missing a blackjack dealer. 'Bout so tall. Well-manicured hands. Good for dealing cards. Better place a help wanted ad in the *Chronicle*. He won't be coming to work anytime soon.

GUTTMANN: Indeed. Until tonight then, sir.

(He throws his head back, laughing, and exits. The GUNSEL hangs back a moment, eyeing FIBONACCI, but then follows his boss. The scene is now the San Francisco piers.)

FIBONACCI (*To the audience.*) And that's how I found myself on the pier in the middle of the night. I didn't like the way things were going. I didn't like being lied to. So, I made a couple of phone calls, and then it was time to test my theory.

(*BROOKE hurries out onto pier and runs over to FIBONACCI.*)

BROOKE: Oh, Philip, there you are. Have you found the nautilus?

FIBONACCI: Yeah, you'd like that, wouldn't you?

BROOKE: I don't know what you mean.

FIBONACCI: You'd better start talking, angel, and make it good.

BROOKE: Philip, please . . .

FIBONACCI: Tears won't work this time, sister. I want answers and I want them now! What's this about the nautilus being the key to your father's code? And how does Guttmann know about it? And what are you doing here when I told you to stay put until I called you?

BROOKE: I was worried about you, Philip. I couldn't sit at home waiting, all the while knowing you'd be meeting the blackmailer here alone.

FIBONACCI: Oh, you're good, sweetheart. But I'm not falling for it this time.

BROOKE: But it's the truth.

(*GUTTMANN and the GUNSEL enter from the shadows. The GUNSEL holds a gun.*)

GUTTMANN: You're wise not to believe her, sir. Her words mean nul.

BROOKE: Guttmann!

GUTTMANN: Miss Taylor. A good evening to you both. Now, Mr. Fibonacci, I believe you said you could produce the nautilus.

BROOKE: You have it?

(*EMMY enters with a bundle.*)

FIBONACCI: Right on time, angel.

EMMY: Here you go, Phil.

GUTTMANN: At last!

FIBONACCI: We never did agree on a figure.

GUNSEL (*Pointing his gun at FIBONACCI.*) Not so fast, college boy.

FIBONACCI: Don't wave that iron at me, kid. It makes me nervous. And I don't like being nervous.

GUTTMANN: You'll excuse me, sir, but I do believe Max and I have the upper hand here. I don't think we need a financial transaction after all.

BROOKE: You're not taking that shell.

FIBONACCI: I have to agree with her.

GUNSEL: Go ahead. Make me use this.

> (*The GUNSEL advances, menacing them with the gun. EMMY pretends to faint, and FIBONACCI uses the distraction to attack the GUNSEL. They struggle. The gun goes off and the GUNSEL slowly crumples to the ground. BROOKE picks up the package. FIBONACCI turns on her.*)

FIBONACCI: Hold it right there, sweetheart.

BROOKE: What are you doing? You won't shoot me. You love me.

FIBONACCI: You're making a big mistake. I was a soldier in the Pacific theater. Without your father's code we'd have been cut to ribbons by the Japanese. I'm not letting this go to the Reds.

BROOKE: You've got it all wrong. That was his plan. Not mine.

GUTTMANN: By gad, you're a liar!

> (*HOBSON, a police detective enters, gun drawn.*)

HOBSON: All right, nobody move.

GUTTMANN: And who is this now?

HOBSON: You can call me Detective Hobson. Badge number sixty-seven, sixty-five, if that helps.

FIBONACCI: Good thing you got here when you did, Hobson.

HOBSON: I came as soon as I got your call. What've we got?

FIBONACCI: I'll tell you the whole story on the way to the precinct.

GUTTMANN: It seems you have bisected our plans by introducing several variables, sir. Well played. I like a man who knows how to use an antiderivative.

FIBONACCI: And I never know what you're talking about. Let's go.

BROOKE: Not me, Philip. You can't . . .

FIBANACCI: Oh, but I can. You're taking the fall, Brooke.

> *(EMMY unwraps the newspaper covered object, revealing a golden nautilus shell. FIBONACCI takes it in his hands.)*

HOBSON: So, this is what it's all about, huh? What is it?

FIBONACCI: It's the stuff that constant recursive integer sequences are made of.

> *(HOBSON waves his gun and ushers BROOKE and GUTTMANN off. FIBONACCI and EMMY follow.)*

BLACK HOLE ENTERPRISES

by C.J. Ehrlich

Original production by
Renegade Theatre Festival
Renegade N.O.W. 2018, Awkward Encounters
August 17–18, 2018
Lansing, MI

Director, Quinn Kelly

ALBI, Max Frutig
RACINE, Anasti Her

Producer, Paige Tufford

CHARACTERS

ALBI, M, age flexible, CEO and founder of Black Hole Enterprises, a
    growing internet-type start-up, about fifty employees.
RACINE, F, 20s, a new hire, eager, upbeat. Three weeks into her new job.

Characters can be of any ethnicity.

SETTING

ALBI'S office, at Black Hole Enterprises.

TIME

TIME

Now.

ALBI, founder of Black Hole Enterprises, sits at his desk, across from his new hire, RACINE. Could be one of those funky, New Age desk situations where at least one person has to sit in some bizarrely uncomfortable position supposed to increase blood flow or something. Long pause.

ALBI: Been having nightmares, Racine? Me calling you in, after just three weeks?

(Laughs; sing-songy.)

Bet you'd like to know why—y.

RACINE (*Hopefully.*) I guess since I'm a newbie it's constructive feedback?

ALBI: I guess since you're a *woman*, it's going to be *very* constructive. So. You liking it here?

RACINE: I'm as happy as possible, sir! . . . OK to use the "H" word?

ALBI: This is a safe space. In here, no one can hear you scream.

(A spooky laugh.)

Just ribbing you.

(With a hard stare.)

Or am I?

(He's not sure.)

Y . . . Yes I am. This job oozes into everything you do. If you're good at it,

RACINE: Oh I get that.

ALBI: Relax. Be yourself! Don't try to act all sad and anxious to impress me! Here, have a lottery ticket.

RACINE: Thanks, sir!

ALBI: It's a loser from yesterday.

RACINE: Awww. (*"I'm losing?"*)

ALBI: There I go again.

RACINE: You're the boss, sir.

ALBI: Sir's my grandfather. I'm the boy genius. Call me Albi. We're family. Going places together.

(He punches her arm.)

Punch Buggy red!

RACINE: Y'know, with my degree in medieval Dutch poetry and Kabuki theatre, my parents never stop telling me I'll end up driving an Uber until I die single and penniless.

ALBI: Cool your jets. You already got the job.

RACINE (*Laughs.*) We don't even have Uber in Little Rock!

ALBI: Everyone's mentioned that about you, uh . . . Uh—

(He consults a clipboard.)

. . . Racine. That way you flip from cheerfully optimistic to self-loathing and insecure in almost the same breath.

RACINE: A steep learning curve but—

ALBI: Exquisite. And by the way, of course I know your name. This . . .

(Clipboard gesture.)

. . . is just a trick of the trade. You felt rotten, right?

RACINE: For a sec!

ALBI: And this.

(He puts his feet up, reads a newspaper, or plays a phone game, ignores her.)

RACINE (*Trying to get his attention.*)
That's what I love about this place! Trying to hold onto your sanity and humanity while—(*She wins.*)
—doling out negativity and aggression on social media? That emotional roller coaster, it's electric!

ALBI: Like grabbing a live wire. And who cut that wire?

RACINE: "I blame the Lizard People!" As my avatar "Merlin" says.

ALBI: I don't know if it's talent, or Bob, but your productivity is exceptional. Most trainees take on six, maybe eight avatars their first month. You've already created ten? And 1,200 posts? Or, somebody's lying.

RACINE: Truth! It helps, I'm messed up. I was abused as a child. Love means hate, hate means love, etc. This is me being me, with a bigger footprint.

ALBI: Inner core of fatalism, that's the secret. I went to a very posh university. With all those "Biffs" and "Corkies" and "the Thirds"? Constantly beating myself up for not being born rich. Plus, I smoked a lot of weed, so my grades "didn't reflect my ability." Well, I frickin showed them. We're small now, but poised for a massive buyout. Though . . . how could that possibly happen, Wall Street thinks we're a black-opps astronomy lab. Keeps me up at night.

(Paranoid.)

You don't talk about us, do you? You signed an NDA! Plus, if you're stupid enough to tell people what you really do, they'd call it immoral? Heinous?

RACINE: "Heartless capitalism at its nadir." That's my "Celia Bishop."

ALBI: Actually, I never smoked weed. That's just a reflex, to make you paranoid about smoking weed.

RACINE: I lied. I had a very happy childhood.

ALBI: Always sounds like Opposite Day around here. Y'ever have that? GET OUT OF MY OFFICE. Just kidding. Or am I? See, Opposite Day.

RACINE: Oh, haha. Look what I missed out on. Coming from Arkansas. America's Armpit. Well . . . to be honest, parts of the Ozarks are mind-blowingly beautiful. Sorry. Too much?

ALBI: See, that level of wiffle-waffle, translates into contagious insecurity. One of the reasons you got hired. That and—

(He makes a gesture referencing femininity.)

RACINE: And—

(She fake cries, convincingly.)

ALBI: Yeah, great. Totally irritates your coworkers.

RACINE: (*Fake crying again.*) But—it—keeps me in the moment!

ALBI: Well, do it quieter, and less whiney. We work on keyboards, not the stage.

RACINE: By the way boss, this is Harassment 101.

   (*She imitates the gesture he made.*)

ALBI: Uh-oh. You just called the Big Boss a Neanderthal.

RACINE: Did I? I did.

ALBI: Need inspiration? Try "Dodgeball." Innocent child, brutally attacked in a daily *Lord of the Flies* ritual. Helpless, the gym teacher watching with one eyeball while he does inventory.

RACINE (*Apologetic.*) We had "Funball." She knew us all by name.

ALBI: Fine. Give up cronuts. Or sushi. Or gluten. Dwell upon it. Your deprivation and suffering.

RACINE: Those are luxuries 99% of the world will never see.

ALBI: "Sexual harassment" then? He said she said. So unfair.

RACINE: It was different in your day.

ALBI: My day? How old do you think I am?—Oho! Very good. Well. As I say, you're doing an exemplary job.

RACINE: Great!

ALBI: Almost too perfect. Your coworkers are jealous.

RACINE: Is that . . . good?

ALBI: For the bottom line. Not for you. Y'oughta hear what they say behind your back.

RACINE (*Frustrated.*) Awww

ALBI: But! But but! (*Ominous pause.*) You know what's coming?

RACINE: No. Maybe.

ALBI (*Sing-songy.*) I can see right through you.

RACINE: Was it, oh. That "Cat Stuck Up a Tree" repost?

ALBI: These don't mention cat.

RACINE: Bob told me that's the term we use.

ALBI: Really . . . ? Bob never told me that.

RACINE: Uh oh. FOMO! "Fear of Missing"—

ALBI: I know!

RACINE: "Cat Stuck Up a Tree", soon as you see the headline, you know the cat's gonna be rescued.

ALBI: You posted a warm and fuzzy?!

RACINE: It's the Girl Scout story, isn't it. These adorable, hearing-impaired ten year olds—

　　(ALBI groans.)

—sold cookies, using sign language, to commuters. Made hundreds.

ALBI: And those selfish moppets blew it on pizza?

RACINE (*A reluctant confession.*) They gave the money to an interfaith—
　　(*Cutting him off.*)—and atheist—initiative to save the homeless from freezing to death.

ALBI: DO YOU NOT UNDERSTAND WHAT WE DO HERE!?

RACINE: I was having an off day. The night before, Cooper whisked me to the top of the Empire State Building. Just us. And the stars. And the glittering lights of the world's greatest city! Then he got on one knee, and proposed.

ALBI: We're not inhuman. I'll chalk it up to the hangover.

RACINE: Hungover on joy and gratitude, you mean. I felt like every choice, every struggle I'd ever risen above led me to that blessed moment.

ALBI: Keep it office appropriate, would you!

RACINE: He runs the travel division at E-Mox.

ALBI: Oh no no. E-Mox is our biggest client. That's collusion.

RACINE: I'm not sure that means what you think it means.

ALBI: You start associating this job with the man you love, dot dot dot. Did Bob train you at all? Horror, not happiness!

RACINE: But . . . my job is to suck people into a dark emotional abyss, until they're so full of existential despair they click on E-Mox vacation ads. Free honeymoon!

ALBI: Don't drag your happy home into my office.

RACINE: I'm very compartmentalized. The only decorations in my cube are stock photos of women laughing while eating salad. It's oppressively cheerful.

ALBI: Tell me about your avatars.

RACINE: They're all self-absorbed, with dozens of IRL frenemies. While most people are on their first social media break, Iggy's still staring at his closet, until he finally picks the same black outfit he wears every day, which reeks of lost opportunity. Chanika and Frank break up every few hours, forcing their friends to take sides. And Angelo. How can one man have so many bad meals at Applebee's?

ALBI: But are they Influencers?

RACINE: I'm most proud of Monique. She's all over her local "moms" group—6000 members—with passive aggressive remarks about burnt-out bulbs and peeling paint and dripping faucets and how much her husband loves watching football.

ALBI: Your politics? Venomous and always right?

RACINE: Merlin's a troll. But so inept! He posts something crazily out of step with whatever forum he's on. Then gets pathetically hurt by the inevitable attacks.

ALBI: Two hits in one.

RACINE: See, that's the crying. It gives me gloom to spare.

ALBI: I have to say, aside from that Girl Scout homeless cat thing, which I have red-flagged, your content's right on the mark. There's a click frenzy on sunny Bahamas vacations, discount cases of single-malt, and that whole Clickbait Your Way to a Flat Stomach maze—! Terrific numbers. You could be management material.

RACINE (*Proudly, in the company spirit.*) "If I wanted to stay in this crap hole."

ALBI: In six months, I can see you really demoralizing a group.

RACINE: "And you'll pay me a shit-ton more. Or I'll sue you."

ALBI: Or you can do fieldwork, sweetie. Wear tight leather skirts in bars, shoot down men who hit on you.

RACINE: No, really. I will sue you. For that alone.

ALBI: Awww.

RACINE: You're such a fricken sexist, Albi. And I'm pretty sure it's illegal to punish me for my fiancé's job.

ALBI: Of course it is!

RACINE: Seriously. I'll OWN this company.

ALBI: We may branch into music. Playlists for department stores, so dismal you have to either buy something or kill yourself . . . Tempting?

RACINE: I'm going straight to HR to file a complaint. Yeah! It will make me worried sick I've shot my career in the foot.

ALBI: Sure, you go overthink that. But first make us the best underground sales force in the universe.

(*They shake. She pointedly wipes her hand on her clothes. He laughs.*)

RACINE: Have a lousy day, sir.

ALBI: Sir's my grand— Oh, hoho!

(*They both laugh.*)

And when I cut you in the lunch line, like I never met you? Just my way of saying "Welcome to Black Hole."

(*RACINE gives him the two finger "I'm watching you" sign as she leaves. He gives it right back.*)

GODDAMMIT INDIRA, where's my next appointment?

BRICKWORK

by K.L. Snodgrass

Production by
Boston Theater Marathon
Sunday, May 6, 2018

Director, Melia Bensussen

STEVIE, John Greene
ITALY, Felix Teich
GARTH, Robert Walsh
SOPRANO, Sarah Joyce Cooper
PIANIST, Nathan Urdangen

CHARACTERS

GARTH, 50s, Boston Southie through and through, gruff, carrying a secret grief.
ITALY, 20s, Italian, accented English, needs harmony, a caretaker.
STEVIE, 30s, Boston Southie, talkative know-it-all but soft underneath, nephew to Garth, in grief as well.
SOPRANO, The voice of an angel, never seen.
PIANIST, if necessary for soprano's warm-ups, never seen.

TIME

February in Boston, after lunch.

SETTING

Newly renovated theater space still in construction.

In the darkness we hear a SOPRANO warming up with scales—this will be heard off and on throughout the play. Lights up on a newly renovated theatre space in Boston. It is daytime in winter, after lunch. Two bricklayers—STEVIE leading ITALY—enter with buckets, brushes, and drop cloths which they proceed to contend with during this first dialogue.

STEVIE: They had to scoop the skeletons out when we started reconstruction! There were, like, I dunno, forty of 'em!

ITALY: *In vero?*

STEVIE: Yeah, sealed up in this wall, and some of 'em . . . had no heads.

> (*He makes a slicing gesture at his neck and a sound.*)

ITALY: (*Crossing himself.*) *Madre del dio.* This is a haunted place.

STEVIE: So now we gotta seal this piece-of-shit wall. Geez, they could cure cancer with this much money, but no (*He makes fun—swaggering, all girly-like.*)
   . . . No, "it's gonna be a *theatre*, and we gotta do somethin' *arty*." Stupid!

> (*He sets down his bucket and starts to throw down the tarpaulin. They hear the SOPRANO singing scales.*)

ITALY: It's a school, no?

STEVIE: Theatre, school, beats me. You seen that big auditorium? They're paintin' with gold in there!

> (*To the ceiling, an order.*) Hey, cure hunger instead, why don'tcha! N'other theatre, my ass. (*At the brick wall.*) But would'ya look at this freakin' mess! (*Beat. To ITALY .*)

Come on, start here about six feet up and move down and over. We'll head toward the windows.

ITALY (*Pointing at the windows.*) Hey, it's snowing!

STEVIE: Ah, crap.

> (*GARTH enters. He's got a bucket, too, which he sets down.*)

GARTH: Ya' got another brush?

STEVIE: Hey, Uncle G., you got some plastic tarp I can use for my car window? The back one's out, and I gotta put something up before—

GARTH: No, I got no "plastic tarp!" You should'a thought of that at lunchtime. You're not puttin' no Saran Wrap on your window now. You're workin'.

(He takes the brush from ITALY and shows him.) Italy, see where they stopped with the sealant? Go up about six feet and get into—

STEVIE (*Overlapping.*) —I told him already—

GARTH (*Ignoring STEVIE.*)—the brick with the brush, like this—don't miss no nook or cranny—

ITALY: Nook or—

GARTH: Don't miss nothin'. We'll each take a six by six, and then we'll move on.

(To STEVIE.)

Ya' bring me a brush, Stevie? (*Beat.*) Figures.

(He exits. STEVIE and ITALY begin to dip their brushes in the clear liquid.)

STEVIE: My Aunt Mary died last month, and he's pissed off ever since. They never had any kids or nothin' so . . .

(Beat. Noticing the bricks.)

Hey, would'ya look at this? It's a name. Yeah, this brick's got a *name* on it, carved like. Would you believe . . . ? F. R. A. . . . Frank This brick's named Frank! See?

(GARTH reenters carrying a new brush.)

ITALY (*Reading the brick.*) *Ef-fe. Er-ray.* . . . Maybe it's the brickmaker.

GARTH: (*With a brush.*) Yeah, or maybe it's "Saran Wrap" seeing things. Get to work and stop reading the bricks.

STEVIE: No lie, Uncle G., it's says "Frank."

GARTH (*Dipping his brush and painting.*) I don't give a crap, keep sealing.

ITALY: Yes, Mister Garth.

STEVIE (*Sotto voce.*) Yeah, yeah.

> (*SILENCE. We hear the SOPRANO warming up with a piano playing scales in another room.*)

ITALY: They doing a *concerto*?

STEVIE: Who knows, they're everywhere—actors, singers, they prolifigate (*sic*) like bugs. I saw a sword fight the other day. They're everywhere—

GARTH: Could'ya keep your thoughts to yourself, please?

STEVIE: Hey, I'm just saying . . . ! (*Sotto voce to ITALY.*) Like I said.

ITALY: She sings pretty. My mother sang in the *Fenice.* (*STEVIE looks.*) *Il teatro.* She sang in the chorus of *Carmen.*

STEVIE: No shit? Hey, Aunt Mary used to sing, didn't she, Uncle G.
   (*He sings.*) "O solo mio . . ." (*sic*).

GARTH: Do I gotta sit on you guys or what? You need reporting?

STEVIE: I can talk and seal, too, you know! (*GARTH gives him a look.*) Okay, okay.

ITALY: Sorry, Mister Garth.

> (*SILENCE. The SOPRANO begins to sing Mimi's Aria from Puccini's La Bohème. Their dialogue flows over it.*)

SOPRANO: (*Offstage.*)
Si, Mi chiamano Mimi,
ma il mio nome è *breve;*
La storia mia è *breve;*

A tela o a seta   ITALY: That is Mimi! I know this.

ricamo in casa e fuori . . .   STEVIE: You know that girl?
Son tranquilla e lieta

ed è *mio svago far gigli e rose.*   ITALY: No, no, but *mia madre* sang
Mi piaccion quelle cose   this song at home.

che han sì dolce malìa,	(*He begins to translate.*) She says . . .
che parlano d'amor, di primavera,	"They always called me Mimi, but my real name is Lucia."
di sogni e di chimere,	STEVIE: (*Laughing.*)
quelle cose che han nome poesia . . .	Geez, that's close—Mimi, Lucia, same diff? Hah!
Lei m'intende?	ITALY: "I sew the . . . " not sure . . . "I sew the cloths at my home, I have a quiet, happy life, and I . . . I garden, I make lilies and roses."

STEVIE: My Aunt Mary had a garden, only she grew onions and stuff. I helped her put river stones around it.

ITALY: " . . . They speak of love, of spring, of dreams and visions . . ."

STEVIE: She didn't have no flowers, but the tomatoes—

(*GARTH throws down his paintbrush.*)

GARTH: I gotta piss.

(*He exits.*)

STEVIE: My aunt used to go to shows sometimes, but he never would. He was pissed off when she went without him, and he's pissed off now. He's gonna spend his life pissed off. And now he's pissing! Hah! Get it?

ITALY: She has a beautiful voice, this *studente*.

STEVIE: Wonder if she's got big bazookas. (*Beat.*) You know, like . . .

(*He gestures—ITALY looks.*)

Oh, I mean, not your mom, nothing like that. I was just—I mean—My Aunt Mary was tiny, so . . . Sorry.

ITALY: The snow killed Mimì .

STEVIE: Yeah, and now it's snowin' in my back seat.

ITALY: She died of . . . what is . . . *consumo*?

STEVIE: My aunt died of cancer. He didn't let nobody in at the end. Only him. Imagine her alone with that angry S.O.B. And she didn't just grow onions, I mean, she could make you laugh . . . ! (*Beat.*) Selfish bastard.

ITALY: *Mia madre*, she is coming to visit us in the spring. Maybe I will bring her to hear the *studenti*.

STEVIE: Yeah, take her to that big gold room. (*GARTH reenters, picking up his brush and painting. To GARTH.*) That was fast.

GARTH: What?

STEVIE: I said, you pee quick.

GARTH: Whadda you care?

STEVIE: I don't.

GARTH: Then shut your trap and get to work.

STEVIE: Always gotta be the boss, right?

GARTH: I AM the boss, and—

ITALY (*Interjecting.*) Mister Garth, this wall had *bodies* in it!

GARTH: —what I say . . . !
      (*To ITALY.*) What?

ITALY: Yes, many bodies from La Mafia killing people.

GARTH: Where'd you hear that?

ITALY: I . . . I . . .

STEVIE: Big John said they found hundreds of skeletons when they—

GARTH: There's no skeletons in this building, ya' idiot! You lookin' for bodies, go visit Somerville.

STEVIE: Big John said—

GARTH: Don't you know when you're being razzed?

   (*The SOPRANO begins to sing the following under the dialogue.*)

SOPRANO (*Offstage.*)

Sono andati? Fingevo
di dormire perché volli
con te sola restare.
Ho tante cose che ti voglio
dire, o una sola,
ma grande come il mare,
come il mare profonda ed infinita . . .
Sei il mio amore e tutta la mia vita!

STEVIE: I'm just saying—

GARTH: Well, quit saying. Use your head and SHUT UP! (*Beat.*) Now, both of ya, GET BACK TO WORK!

> (*Silence. STEVIE picks up his brush. Then looks at the wall, and with deliberation.*)

STEVIE: Hey, would you looky here.

GARTH: What now?

STEVIE: This brick's got another name.

ITALY: "Frank"?

STEVIE: No. No, it's an "M" . . . "A" . . . "R" . . . Yeah, it's Mary! This brick is named MARY—

> (*GARTH drops his brush and moves to STEVIE, pulling him by the shirt, threatening, powerful. STEVIE fights back—he's hoping for it. They scuffle.*)

GARTH: Come on, you little shit! You want to say something? Spit it out!

STEVIE: You wouldn't let us in the room! Why wouldn't you let me in—?

GARTH: You come in the room when I say so!

STEVIE: I didn't get to say goodbye!

GARTH: Yeah, well maybe she didn't want you there—

STEVIE: She loved me, too!

GARTH: —did ya' think of that?

STEVIE: I could have been there to—to—

GARTH: To what? To what?

STEVIE: I could have been there—

GARTH: Be sure she's dead?

STEVIE: —to help YOU!

ITALY: Mary!

> *(GARTH and STEVIE turn to look.)*

She is singing again. She is saying . . . "Have they gone? I only pretended to be asleep because I wanted to be left alone with you."

> *(In time, GARTH moves back, lets go of STEVIE and listens. STEVIE watches.)*

GARTH: Mary, she . . . ! How did you know—? She said—?

ITALY: "I have many things I want to tell you, but in truth only one. It is as grand as the sea, as deep and as infinite."
> *(They all listen.)* "You are my entire life, you are my love."

SOPRANO:	ITALY:
Piangi?	"Are you crying?
Sto bene.	"I'm fine."
Pianger così, perché?	"Why do you cry like this?"
Qui . . . amor . . .	"Here . . . my love . . . "
. . . sempre con te!	" . . . always with you!"
Le mani . . .	"My hands . . . "
al caldo . . .	"in the warm . . .
e . . . dormire . . .	"and to sleep . . . "
(As the song ends.)	
Silenzio.	
(Pause.)	

STEVIE: I loved her, too.

GARTH: I know. (*Beat.*) I know.

> *(He turns and pulls STEVIE to his breast. They stand in grief, together.)*

ITALY: *Mia madre* sang that song at home.

> *(When he must, GARTH pats STEVIE on the cheek and lets him go.)*

GARTH (*Gathering himself.*) Okay. Enough. We gotta seal this wall.

> *(He returns to his bucket and picks up his brush. ITALY and STEVIE do the same. Beat.)*

I uh . . . I got some plastic tarp in my truck. I'll fix the window, Stevie.
> *(He sets down his brush, saying.)* When I get back, we'll start in the other direction. (*Beat, as he exits.*) And NO YAPPIN'!

> *(ITALY and STEVIE turn back to the sealing of the wall. ITALY glances at the windows.)*

ITALY: Look! It's snowing again.

STEVIE: Yeah. Snow.

> *(Beat. He looks toward the SOPRANO's direction.)*

Snow is good.

> *(He stares as lights fade to black.)*

CHARLOTTESVILLE

by Suzanne Bradbeer

Charlottesville was first presented (as *Downtown*) April 26–May 13, 2018, in Dreamcatcher Rep's spring production of short plays entitled *Continuing the Conversation*; Laura Ekstrand, Producing Artistic Director. The play was directed by Harriett Trangucci, the production stage manager was Amy Hadam.

DANI, Noreen Farley
CARRIE ANNE, Beth Painter
SETH, Ben Kaufman

Charlottesville was subsequently produced by Barrington Stage Company as part of their annual 10X10 New Play Festival February 14–March 10, 2019, with Julianne Boyd as Artistic Director. The play was directed by Julianne Boyd, the production stage manager was Renee Lutz.

DANI, Peggy Pharr Wilson
CARRIE ANNE, Keri Safran
SETH, Michael Fell

© 2019 by Suzanne Bradbeer. Reprinted by permission of the author. For performance rights, contact Amy Wagner, Abrams Artists Agency, amy.wagner@ abramsartny.com

CHARACTERS

DANI, 60s–70s, white.
CARRIE ANNE, 30s–40s, white. Dani's daughter.
SETH, 30s–40s, white. Dani's son.

SETTING

A recent August by a lake.

For my hometown

The edge of a lake. DANI sits with her fishing line extending into the water. Both DANI and the fishing line are very still. CARRIE ANNE enters. It is a cloudy August day.

CARRIE ANNE: How many have you caught?

DANI: None.

> *(CARRIE ANNE looks out at the lake, at the day. She looks at DANI who is still sitting, immobile. She looks at the fishing line laying inert in the lake.)*

CARRIE ANNE: I don't know much about fishing but aren't you supposed to—

> *(She mimes casting.)*

—if you're not getting, you know.

DANI: The word is cast.

CARRIE ANNE: Cast, right. Aren't you supposed to—

DANI: I did.

CARRIE ANNE: But I mean—

DANI: That's why it's in the water.

CARRIE ANNE: But then, you do it again, right, if nothing is biting.

DANI (*Nodding at a paper bag nearby.*) There's a biscuit if you want it.

> *(CARRIE ANNE takes a biscuit out of the bag as she tries to figure out how to ease into a conversation she doesn't want to have.)*

CARRIE ANN: What kind of lure are you using?

DANI: I'm using bait, Honey.

CARRIE ANNE: Bait, right. Do you use worms, or . . . ?

DANI: The thing is, I go fishing for the quiet.

(CARRIE ANNE, who finds she has no appetite, puts the biscuit back in the bag. Then:)

CARRIE ANNE: I think Seth was down there on Saturday.

DANI: —

CARRIE ANNE: In the middle of everything. Did he talk to you about it?

DANI: No.

CARRIE ANNE: Well I, I think he—

DANI: He was with me on Friday.

CARRIE ANN: I'm talking about Saturday.

DANI: Oh. Could have been.

CARRIE ANNE: I think he might have been . . . involved.

DANI: What are you getting at?

(CARRIE ANNE takes out her phone. She shows DANI a photo.)

Why are you showing me that?

CARRIE ANNE: They're looking for the people who were beating on that kid. I think Seth was one of them.

DANI: Why would he be beating on that kid?

CARRIE ANNE: Why would anyone?

DANI *(Of the photo.)* I don't see him.

CARRIE ANNE: Look at the guy behind the guy in the camo jacket.

DANI: He doesn't own a camo jacket.

CARRIE ANNE: No, behind him; the guy in the orange hat behind the camo guy. He's mostly blocked, but that's Seth's arm and that is his hat.

DANI: I've never seen that hat.

CARRIE ANNE: You've haven't seen all his clothes, Mom! I mean, I know you still do his laundry but—

DANI: Where did you get that picture?

CARRIE ANNE: Twitter.

DANI: *Twitter.*

CARRIE ANNE: They're looking for the people who did it. They're asking the public to come forward if they recognize—

DANI: Who's asking? The Tweeter people?

CARRIE ANNE: It's, yes, people on Twitter are trying to identify the five men beating on that kid.

DANI: Hold on, hold on—you want to turn in your brother to, to *Twitter?*

CARRIE ANNE: No, I don't, but—

DANI: You want to turn in your brother—your *brother*—on the basis of an orange hat?!

CARRIE ANNE: Not just the hat—

DANI: Not to mention Seth would never wear an orange hat, he looks terrible in orange, you both do, neither of my children should ever wear orange and I say that with love.

CARRIE ANNE: Mom, you recognize your own son, I know you do.

DANI: It is impossible to identify a person based on that little bit of blurry nothing! He doesn't know those people, I'm sure he was nowhere near that group.

CARRIE ANNE: Let's ask him.

DANI: We are not asking him and we are not accusing him, he is barely keeping himself together! He's looking for work, he needs his confidence. But I'll tell you this: Seth is not a racist.

CARRIE ANNE: —

DANI: When Seth was in the sixth grade his best friend was Tyree Washington. And when Tyree was walking home one day, a bunch of white kids cornered him behind the 7-11, and, and someone took out a knife! Tyree started to cry and that's when Seth! Yes, Seth! Came flying out of the 7-11! He started picking boys off Tyree, just picking them up and tossing them aside. Tyree talked to me later, he thanked me later! He said it was like Seth were some kind of superhero flying in and saving him.

CARRIE ANNE: I remember that story.

DANI: It's not a story! It's what happened.

CARRIE ANNE: I'm sure it is, but—

DANI: You listen to me! Your brother is not a racist! His best friend was Tyree Washington!

CARRIE ANNE (*Gently.*) So what happened to him, Mom? Because he's changed.

DANI: It's these outsiders, they come to our town and cause all this trouble. There is a girl dead, there are two cops dead there was just a lot of bad all the way round and now it's time for everyone to just go back to where they came from and leave us be!

CARRIE ANNE (*Holding up her phone.*) I can't look at this photo/ and not—

DANI: It's all because of that statue—which has been there for a hundred years—that statue wasn't hurting anyone! But that girl, that little black girl at CHS, started a petition, said it's offensive, said she's uncomfortable by it, said she and her friends don't go to that park because of it—well, grow up kid, nobody goes to that park, it's not even a park! It's a little slip of land with a statue on it that no one ever noticed! But no, she was made uncomfortable and look what it led to!

CARRIE ANNE: But Mom—

DANI: My boy is not like that, he is just not like that and that's not him in the picture.

(*SETH appears with a fishing rod.*)

SETH: Yo, Sis! When did you get to town? Mom, you're in my spot. Just kidding.
(*He sweeps over to DANI, kissing her on the cheek.*) Everything okay with you?

DANI: There's a biscuit in that bag.

SETH: Carrie, check it

> *(He comes right up close to CARRIE ANNE. A little too close. CARRIE ANNE rears back a little.)*

Easy, it's just me.

CARRIE ANNE: Check what?

SETH: My new friend.

> *(He holds out his finger. CARRIE ANNE leans in cautiously.)*

CARRIE ANNE: . . . What, is it?

SETH: It's a leafhopper. A Candy-Striped Leafhopper.

CARRIE ANNE: Do they bite?

SETH: No.

> *(The leafhopper jumps on CARRIE ANNE's arm. She gasps.)*

SETH: But they jump.

> *(CARRIE ANNE laughs in spite of herself. We don't need to see the bug but we need to believe that CARRIE ANNE and SETH see it.)*

Ralph, say hi to my sister.

CARRIE ANNE: He's pretty cute.

SETH: Leafhoppers are the cutest. The leafhopper's Latin name *Bellus Floridus* means "cutest bug."

CARRIE ANNE: Really?

SETH: No.

CARRIE ANNE: Uh-oh.

DANI: What?

CARRIE ANNE: I think Ralph just pooped on me.

SETH: Ralph! Give him.

> *(He puts out his arm to let the bug jump back on. It does.)*

Yo, Ralph, not cool, so not cool, man.

(He gently wipes the "poop" from his sister's arm.)

Sorry about that.

DANI/CARRIE ANNE: Not your fault.

(The leafhopper flies off.)

SETH: Adios, Ralph, give my regards to the fam!
(To CARRIE ANNE.) Sit down, take your shoes off, the sun'll be back out soon, it's going to be a pretty one.

(As he gets his fishing rod ready.)

I bet you're glad you weren't around for all the crazy last weekend.

DANI: Leave it alone, Seth.

CARRIE ANNE: Were you there, did you go downtown?

SETH: Hell yeah, I went downtown. I'm not letting my man Lee go down without a word. I mean, why's everyone bashing on Robert E. Lee these days? Doesn't seem right to treat an American hero like that. Lee was a man of his time. A man of his time who tried to do right by his people. Meaning Virginians, we're his people.

DANI: Why won't either of you eat your biscuit?

SETH: I tip my hat to Robert E. Lee and I'm not ashamed to say it.

DANI: It's your favorite, the one with the cheese baked in.

SETH: Anyone want to defend General Sherman? But nobody's taking down his statues. It's just bullshit, it's all bullshit. You know what I hear all the time now? White men this and white men that. I lost my job to a guy who was black; he had less experience than I did but when it came down to laying people off, they kept him! You don't think that's racism? That's racism! But no, we're not allowed to say that, black folks can't be racist. I got shoved around at a game last spring by some black dudes—

DANI: Leave it alone, would you please!

SETH: But it was fine! That's the point! They liked Carolina, I liked Virginia, and we got a little physical, but we didn't call each other racists! We just liked different teams and it got a little heated and then it was done. But now you can't express your opinion, you can't! If you're white, you're damned if you do and damned if you don't. It's bullshit, man, it is Bull. Shit.

CARRIE ANNE: Did you hear about that kid?

SETH: What kid?

CARRIE ANNE: This black kid, he got beaten up by a mob, broken ribs, a concussion. He's still in the hospital.

DANI: There are a lot of people in the hospital right now.

CARRIE ANNE: This was a particular kid, early 20's, it was by First Wachovia Bank—

SETH: The whole thing was chaos.

CARRIE ANNE: He was beaten up.

SETH: That's what you keep saying. Do you know him or something?

CARRIE ANNE: Me? No, I—

SETH: Because you don't actually know any black kids, do you? But sure, come back down here and start complaining about a troublemaker who got himself a little roughed up.

CARRIE ANNE: Why do you say troublemaker?

(DANI starts reeling in her fishing line.)

SETH: 'Cause I heard about it, okay, everybody heard about it.

DANI: If you don't stop talking about that mess I'm going to throw myself in the lake, just throw myself in!

SETH: You're upsetting Mom. And with everything she's been through, too.

CARRIE ANNE: I thought everything was fine.

SETH: It's fine *now*, but she didn't tell you the half of it, all the tests, because she doesn't like to worry you.

CARRIE ANNE: Mom?

(DANI dismisses the subject with a wave of her hand.)

Oh my God, this *family*!

> *(The sun comes out from behind the clouds. CARRIE ANNE shades her eyes with her hand.)*

SETH: Hello sun! I knew you would come out!

CARRIE ANNE: I'm going back to the house.

SETH: See you at dinner.

> *(CARRIE ANNE exits without responding. SETH pulls out an orange UVA baseball hat and puts it on to shield his eyes. He opens his tackle box.)*

DANI: Where did you get that hat?

SETH: This? It's a common UVA hat and I went to UVA, what about it?

DANI: I've never seen it before.

SETH: It's a common hat.

DANI: Give it to me.

SETH: What, why?

DANI: Give it to me!

> *(She grabs the hat and stuffs it in a pocket.)*

SETH: What the hell, Mom!

> *(DANI goes to leave, then turns back a moment.)*

DANI: You were best friends with Tyree Washington.

> *(They stare at each other a moment, then DANI exits. SETH looks out at the lake.)*

CODE

by Andrea Fleck Clardy

Originally produced by
Ixion Ensemble
Lansing MI
May 12–20, 2018

EVANS, Sadonna Croff
SMITHSON, Danica O'Neill
MALE VOICE, Ben Guenther

CHARACTERS

EVANS, The project manager in a government office, dressed plainly in
    dark colors, in her fifties.
SMITHSON, A computer programmer who reports to EVANS, in her
    thirties.

Lights up on a sparsely furnished office space, with door upstage right, desk downstage left. The desk has a phone and a computer on it, a facing chair for visitors.

The time is 2035, when offices and residences everywhere in the United States have been fitted with recording microphones. Through surveillance programs that code "illegal or immoral content," the government monitors all conversations. This is the department in which the surveillance programs are written and revised. EVANS sits at her desk, working. We hear a knock on an unseen door. EVANS reaches over to push a button before she speaks.

EVANS: Yes?

SMITHSON: (*From offstage.*) It's Smithson.

EVANS: Come in.

(*SMITHSON enters.*)

SMITHSON: Want to let you know I'm going out at lunchtime.

EVANS: (*Still working as she speaks.*) I wouldn't do that.

SMITHSON: Why not?

EVANS: The demonstrations have started.

SMITHSON: Exactly.

EVANS: You have forty minutes for lunch, Smithson.

SMITHSON: I know.

EVANS: You'll never make your way through the crowds, eat your lunch, and get back in time.

SMITHSON: I'll skip the lunch.

EVANS: You'll still take more than forty minutes.

SMITHSON: I'll make the time up at the end of the day.

EVANS: Besides, we have a meeting at one o'clock.

SMITHSON: What meeting?

EVANS: You and I need to meet.

SMITHSON: You hadn't told me.

EVANS: I'm telling you now. One o'clock. Here in my office.

SMITHSON: Could we just meet now?

EVANS: No. I'm busy now.

(*Beat.*)

SMITHSON: Evans, will you come with me to the demonstration?

(*EVANS stops working.*)

EVANS: What?

SMITHSON: Come with me. Then you'll see for yourself. You'll feel different. I know you will.

EVANS: Out of the question.

SMITHSON: (*Moving closer, speaking more softly.*) Remember the Chicago conference we went to when I was new? Remember the rally outside our hotel, how we felt when we watched it together?

EVANS: I remind you, Smithson, that no conversation is private.

SMITHSON: Right. The slogan we're releasing next week says: "You never need to feel alone. We are listening for your sake."

EVANS: This office is like every other office in that regard. All the rules apply.

SMITHSON: Of course.

EVANS: Don't be late for our meeting.

SMITHSON: There's something else.

EVANS: Can it wait?

SMITHSON: No.

EVANS: I'm very busy.

SMITHSON: You're always busy.

EVANS: What then?

SMITHSON: About the new program. . .

EVANS: (*Meeting SMITHSON'S eyes for the first time.*) Be careful.

SMITHSON: The new . . .

EVANS: We cannot discuss the new program.

SMITHSON: Okay. Okay. Listen, Evans, please. Can we talk about the new . . . recipe?

EVANS: The new recipe?

SMITHSON: Yes.

EVANS: It looks delicious, doesn't it?

SMITHSON: I can't cook that recipe.

EVANS: Of course you can.

SMITHSON: No.

EVANS: I know you, Smithson. I taught you how to cook. You're doing very well. I'm pleased with what you prepare.

SMITHSON: I can't.

EVANS: Can't what?

SMITHSON: I can't be responsible for more people . . .

EVANS: Stop. We are talking about an interesting recipe. We are talking about making soup.

SMITHSON: I'm telling you that cooking this new soup is impossible for me. How can I explain this to you, Evans? I don't mind peeling potatoes. I don't mind chopping carrots. But this recipe starts with a live chicken. A creature with a warm body and a beating heart. I can't do it. I can't wring the necks of any more chickens.

EVANS: What?

SMITHSON: I can't wring . . .

EVANS: I heard what you said. Very theatrical. Very vivid. Let me remind you that your hands are clean. You are a technician. You never hear a squawk. You never touch a feather. You see no blood at all.

SMITHSON: But I know what happens. I think about. . .

EVANS: Stop thinking those thoughts. You have a job to do. It's that simple.

SMITHSON: It's no longer simple for me. It's dark and complex.

EVANS: We've worked together for six years, Smithson. I know what you are capable of doing. You're the best programmer I've trained.

SMITHSON: I can't sleep. When I finally fall asleep, I wake up in the middle of the night, my heart pounding.

EVANS: We can fix that.

(Opening her desk drawer, she takes out a pill bottle.)

Take this. Melatonin. It will help you stay asleep.

SMITHSON: Melatonin won't help.

EVANS: Then try Benadryl.

SMITHSON: That's not the point.

EVANS: Of course, it is. You have a pharmaceutical problem. If Benadryl's not strong enough, I'll get you a prescription.

(Beat.)

SMITHSON: Tell me how you keep going, how you keep from wondering . . .

EVANS: Stop talking. Just wait.

(She types something into the computer, pauses, types something more.)

There. I've put a two-minute block on surveillance of this office.

SMITHSON: You've done what?

EVANS: Nobody can hear us now. We have two minutes of privacy.

SMITHSON: I never knew that was possible.

EVANS: Until now, you didn't need to know.

SMITHSON: Two minutes.

EVANS: A little less now.

SMITHSON: Is the code for two minutes of privacy authorized?

EVANS: No.

SMITHSON: So you wrote the script on your own?

EVANS: Obviously.

SMITHSON: Wow. I'm impressed. I'm thrilled, actually. *(Pause.)* We're really alone.

EVANS: For the next minute and twenty-two seconds.

SMITHSON: Help me think, Evans. I can't keep doing this work.

EVANS: (*Gently.*) Yes, you can. I need you here.

(*She takes SMITHSON's hand.*)

SMITHSON: The more they know, the more harm they do. The more people they torture and kill. What happened to Kenyon and Fargo? It's been two months since they disappeared. What happened to them? I heard Pappas was executed. Her books are all gone from the libraries, stripped from the electronic record.

EVANS: Don't think about those people. They made stupid mistakes.

SMITHSON: Nicholas, most of all.

EVANS: Your brother was proud of the work you do.

SMITHSON: I miss him.

EVANS: Think of the new regulations as a programming challenge. That's what Nicholas would have told you. Think of them as a puzzle we are paid to solve. Together. We work well together.

SMITHSON: (*Urgently.*) Somewhere we have to draw the line. A program for subcutaneous monitors goes too far.

EVANS: That's not our call.

SMITHSON: We're letting the government get under our skin. Literally. Under everybody's skin. It's too much. I can't do it.

EVANS: You're upset, Smithson. I understand. But I don't want you to make a huge mistake, a mistake you can never undo. If you refuse to do the work, you'll be reported.

SMITHSON: You won't report me.

EVANS: Refusal at your level is treason. You know what happens.

SMITHSON: I can't keep doing this.

EVANS: Nothing that happens here will change if you leave. They'll hire someone else. That person is not likely to be as skilled as you. But she'll do. I'll train her to write the code and the process will continue.

SMITHSON: Only it won't be on my conscience.

EVANS: At the very least, you will never work again. That means you will never have enough money. You will never have enough food. You will lose forever the luxury of being ignored. You'll be singled out and delayed and harassed. You'll be accused of one thing after another.

SMITHSON: I have to take that chance.

EVANS: That's not a chance, Smithson. It's a certainty. You will make yourself miserable. And for what? What good can you possibly do?

SMITHSON: Saying "no" will do me good.

EVANS: On the contrary, it will do you great harm.

SMITHSON: Listen, Evans. If you could program a surveillance break by yourself, if you could create a two-minute safe space . . .

EVANS: Don't go there.

SMITHSON: Together we could change the code that tracks forbidden behaviors and treasonous impulses. I could stay.

EVANS: Hush.

SMITHSON: Whoever writes the code decides what they know.

EVANS: They know everything.

SMITHSON: Because we let them! What if everybody had a work-around that gave them one hour alone? Or what if a small portion of information is lost in translation to the binary code?

EVANS: Out of the question. There is a limit to what will go unnoticed. Because of my rank, they ignore two minutes of privacy once every few months. Not more.

SMITHSON: We could change that.

EVANS: Wait. Our time is up.

   (She types something into her computer.)

SMITHSON: You gave us two more minutes. Oh, my God. That's wonderful. Thank you, Evans.

(She moves towards EVANS, who stops her with a gesture.)

EVANS: Keep talking.

SMITHSON: I've been thinking of ways we can create gaps.

EVANS: I don't know what you mean.

SMITHSON: We'll build the pipeline with holes. For starters, we drop certain words that trigger investigations, like "sex" and "revolt" and "secret." Then we lock out the input from one microphone in every building to create a small safe place.

EVANS: No.

SMITHSON: Think what it would mean to have a safe place in every building. Workers could organize. Reporters could exchange information. People could read poems or sing songs. Nobody would know what went on. We could do this together, Evans. I know we could.

EVANS: We would be directly violating government intent. That is treason.

SMITHSON: Only if they find out about it.

(Beat.)

EVANS: We don't have time to talk about this now.

SMITHSON: Come out with me at lunchtime. Please.

EVANS: No. We'll meet this afternoon.

SMITHSON: We can talk about this then?

EVANS: Don't be late.

SMITHSON: Thank you, Evans. Oh, my God.

(She laughs a little.)

I'm so relieved. Thank you so much.

EVANS: Don't thank me, Smithson. There is no reason to thank me.

(Knock at the door. EVANS pushes button.)

I'm busy.

MALE VOICE: Evans!

EVANS: What is it?

MALE VOICE: We need Smithson.

EVANS: What do you want with Smithson?

MALE VOICE: She stands accused.

SMITHSON: (*With sudden awful certainty.*) Oh, my God. There was no surveillance break.

MALE VOICE: (*Louder.*) We're coming in.

EVANS: No need to raise your voice. The door is open.

    (*Blackout.*)

DEATH DEFYING

by Stephen Kaplan

Originally performed at
Luna Stage
New Moon Short Play Festival
May 22, 2018

Director, Mikaela Kafka

ZAZEL, Anna Gion
AIRABELLA, Stephanie Windland

CHARACTERS

ZAZEL, female, any age, but older than Airabella. The first human
    cannonball in the world who performed her act in the late 1800s.
AIRABELLA, female, younger than Zazel. A human arrow who performed
    her act for contemporary audiences.

SETTING

A waiting room. Chairs and magazines and a door leading off.

*A waiting room. Chairs and magazines. A closed door leads to another room.
ZAZEL, a woman dressed in a circa-1880 circus leotard, sits. She reads a magazine and quietly hums "Entrance of the Gladiators." AIRABELLA, a younger*

woman dressed in a more contemporary acrobatic circus leotard, enters. She looks around, clearly uncertain of herself or her surroundings.

ZAZEL: Hi.

AIRABELLA: Oh, I'm sorry. I didn't notice you . . . thank you.

(*Looking around.*)

Is there anything I should . . . ?

ZAZEL: Just pull up a chair and wait.

AIRABELLA: OK.

(*She sits. Clearly nervous.*)

ZAZEL: Nice outfit.

AIRABELLA: I'm sorry?

ZAZEL: I said I like your outfit.

AIRABELLA: Oh. Thank you. (*Beat.*) I like yours as well.

ZAZEL: Thanks, but you don't have to say that just because I complimented yours.

AIRABELLA: No. I mean it.

ZAZEL: Because a compliment given only after one received can be seen as disingenuine.

AIRABELLA: I think you mean "disingenuous." (*Beat.*) "Ingenuous" means innocent and unsuspecting so *dis*ingenuous means you thought I was *pretending* to be innocent and unsuspecting. Not "not genuine." Though they share the same root—"gen"—from birth. (*Beat.*) Sorry. I'm into etymology. (*Beat.*) Where words come from?

ZAZEL: You like knowing where things come from?

AIRABELLA: Yes. And I do like your outfit. I wasn't being disin—because I did think, "That's a very nice outfit. It's a shame they don't make them like that anymore." Not that I mean that it's old-timey or anything—I just meant—

ZAZEL: It's OK. You don't need to be nervous.

AIRABELLA: I'm not normally. Can't be in my line of work. I do a pretty dangerous circus act. In fact, that's where the etymology comes in. When I'm preparing, I break down words. Roots—prefixes—suffixes. It calms and focuses me. Keeps me on my best game.

ZAZEL: Doesn't always work though, does it?

AIRABELLA: What do you mean?

ZAZEL: Well . . .

(Gesturing to the room.)

. . . you're here.

AIRABELLA So that means I'm really . . . And you're . . . ?

ZAZEL: I'm . . . ?

AIRABELLA: Isn't there supposed to be some kind of . . . welcoming committee or something?

ZAZEL: You have to wait 'til they call your name.

AIRABELLA: Oh. OK.

ZAZEL: *(Beat.)* Before my act I just focused on my breath to calm me.

AIRABELLA: I knew it! I knew that you must have an act as well!

ZAZEL: Really. What gave it away?

AIRABELLA: Well, your—

(Referencing ZAZEL's outfit.)

What's your act?

ZAZEL: You don't know?

AIRABELLA: No. Should I?

ZAZEL: I was a human cannonball.

AIRABELLA: I'm a human arrow! What are the odds that both of us . . . oh . . . oh . . . so is this place just for . . . ? Wow. That sure is specific.

ZAZEL: So, how did you get into—

AIRABELLA: It's in my blood. My dad did high wire and my mom and grandma did aerial tricks. What about you?

ZAZEL: I just wanted to fly.

AIRABELLA: Yeah. That part rocked. (*Beat.*) How far did you go?

ZAZEL: Oh, we don't need to—

AIRABELLA: I'll tell you mine if you tell me yours.

ZAZEL: It's really not—

AIRABELLA: Come on.

ZAZEL: Twenty feet. (*Beat.*) I know it's not much by today's standards, but—

AIRABELLA: No, it's . . . it's very impressive.

ZAZEL: We were working with rubber springs.

AIRABELLA: Rubber? That's so . . .

ZAZEL: Well, I was the first.

AIRABELLA: The first?

ZAZEL: Yes. Well, some say George and Ella did it, but Ella just caught George, so I was the first woman.

AIRABELLA: Like . . . ever?

ZAZEL: Like . . . yes.

AIRABELLA: That's so cool.

ZAZEL: Thank you. (*Beat.*) And you?

AIRABELLA: Me?

ZAZEL: How far?

AIRABELLA: Oh. Um, a bit.

ZAZEL: A bit.

AIRABELLA: Yeah.

ZAZEL: A bit twenty? A bit thirty?

AIRABELLA: A bit . . . eighty. To ninety. But the crossbow I use is . . . was . . . if I had to use rubber like you, then . . . (*Beat.*) So how long do we wait?

ZAZEL: It depends.

AIRABELLA: How long have you been waiting?

ZAZEL: A bit.

AIRABELLA: A bit twenty? A bit thirty?

ZAZEL: A bit eighty. Eighty-one to be precise.

AIRABELLA: You've been stuck here eighty-one years?

ZAZEL: Yes.

AIRABELLA: (*Looking around.*) Where's everyone else?

ZAZEL: They all got called before me.

AIRABELLA: Why?

ZAZEL: They had their names. You can't go in unless they have your name.

AIRABELLA: So you said. But why don't they have your name?

ZAZEL: Do you know my name?

AIRABELLA: No.

ZAZEL: Why not?

AIRABELLA: I—

ZAZEL: Do you realize that if I hadn't done what I did then you would not have been able to do what you did? That my rubber springs led to your . . . crossbow? That my twenty feet led to your eighty or ninety?

AIRABELLA: No. I didn't.

ZAZEL: What's *your* name?

AIRABELLA: My name? My name's *Air*abella. They came up with it. The marketing team, I mean.

ZAZEL: But that's not your real name, right? They need your real name.

AIRABELLA: Oh. My real name's . . . (*Beat.*) It's— . . .

ZAZEL: Can't remember, can you?

AIRABELLA: I—

ZAZEL: That's what happens when you let them call you something else for so long. You forget, too. (*Silence.*) They called me Zazel.

AIRABELLA: But that's not your real name though?

ZAZEL: Does Zazel sound like a real name?

AIRABELLA: And you don't remember your real name either?

ZAZEL: Bingo.

AIRABELLA: Then how'd the others get in if they didn't know their real names?

ZAZEL: Someone else knew. A friend. Acquaintance. Those interested in the ones that came before. (*Beat.*) And so we wait.

(She goes back to her magazine.)

AIRABELLA: So I have to wait until someone knows my name? My real name.

ZAZEL: Yes.

AIRABELLA: But everyone else—all the other women—someone eventually knew *their* real names, right?

ZAZEL: Eventually.

AIRABELLA: So the odds are in my favor.

ZAZEL: Until they're not. The odds that the net is in the right place. The odds that the mechanism propelling you is well-oiled, well-maintained. The odds that the velocity and distance and weight and acceleration and—

AIRABELLA: —fire extinguishers. (*Beat.*) They set me on fire. When the act got stale, they needed a way to . . . they couldn't put me out.

ZAZEL: I'm sorry.

AIRABELLA: So I'm screwed. The odds are not in my favor and I'm gonna be stuck here forever!

ZAZEL: Like me?

AIRABELLA: I didn't mean—but why the name? Why's that so important?

ZAZEL: Are you Airabella?

AIRABELLA: What do you mean? I told you—

ZAZEL: I mean is that how you'd introduce yourself?

AIRABELLA: That's how they wanted me to—in every interview, I had to—

ZAZEL: But was that who you were?

AIRABELLA: (*Beat.*) No.

ZAZEL: When someone remembers our name, *knows* it, it's a sign that we were there. And then we can live on and keep going. It's our true sense. Our etymology.

AIRABELLA: (*Beat.*) My mother and grandmother used to try to tell me. . . . Wait! Did you meet them? They also . . . were they here?

ZAZEL: Maybe. I . . . There have been so many. I don't remember.

AIRABELLA: Because they would've known my name.

ZAZEL: You were saying they used to try to tell you . . . ?

AIRABELLA: You know. Stories. Before they . . . She and my grandmother would talk about the history, how tricks and styles evolved, but I never . . . I think I was a disappointment to them in that regard. But why focus on the past when you always have to be so in the present, you know?

ZAZEL: I know.

AIRABELLA: I mean our lives depend on it, right? You can't think of the last fly you did or the next one, just—

ZAZEL: —the one you're doing right now.

AIRABELLA: Yes! (*Beat.*) I'm sorry I don't know your name. That I don't know who you are. Or . . . were.

(*Beat.*)

ZAZEL: Thank you.

(Beat. AIRABELLA gestures to the magazines.)

AIRABELLA: So any recommendations which to start with? A particularly engaging article? A crossword puzzle worth—

ZAZEL I've already done them all.

AIRABELLA: Oh.

(Silence as AIRABELLA picks up a magazine and starts to read it. ZAZEL watches her. Then—)

ZAZEL: So I was being disingenuous.

(AIRABELLA looks up.)

That's the word, right? Disingenuous? I know your name.

AIRABELLA: You do?

(ZAZEL nods.)

How?

ZAZEL: For all her interest in history, your grandmother didn't know my name either. She felt bad, too. And so did your mom when she arrived. They, of course, knew each other's names, so . . . And you were not a disappointment to them. They were very, very proud of you. Before their names were called they told me yours. They obviously hoped I wouldn't need it because, well, it would mean you had better odds than the rest of us. But I know your name.

AIRABELLA: Oh.

ZAZEL; I just hoped that maybe you'd . . .

(She smiles sadly.)

Well, one of these days. So your name is—

AIRABELLA: No.

ZAZEL: No?

AIRABELLA: Not yet.

ZAZEL: What do you mean?

AIRABELLA: I've only been here a few minutes. I can wait a little longer with you. If you'd like. (*Beat.*) Maybe the next one'll be a bit more . . . aware than me. (*Silence.*) Tell me about your act.

(*Silence.*)

ZAZEL: My act.

(*She smiles a huge smile.*)

My act was the first of its kind. No one had even thought of it before me.

(*Lights fade as ZAZEL tells her story.*)

ESPERANTO

by Brian Silberman

Produced by
Camino Real Playhouse ShowOff! 2019 Reader's Series
January 10–13, 2019

Director, Felicia Whalen

CHARACTERS

PO, a giant panda, male.
TIAN TIAN, a giant panda, female.

SETTING

An open area in Zoo Atlanta's giant panda enclosure. The present.

The play benefits from a pared-down style of presentation, with minimal scenery, merely a suggestion of space and selected scenic elements, like the pile of woodchips. While the characters are actual Giant Pandas, there are to be no panda costumes or animal ears or noses. At most, actors can wear thick, slightly oversized sweaters (in dark monochromatic colors only). They should not attempt to walk on all fours, but can utilize select, panda-like gestures and movement when appropriate.

I said that I thought the secret of life was obvious: be here now, love as if your whole life depended on it, find your life's work, and try to get hold of a giant panda. If you had a giant panda in your backyard, anything could go wrong—someone could die, or stop loving you, or you could get sick—and if you could look outside and see this adorable, ridiculous, boffo panda, you'd start to laugh; you'd be so filled with thankfulness and amusement that everything would be O.K. again.

—Anne Lamott, *Hard Laughter*

PO and TIAN TIAN, in an open space. PO paces back and forth along an unseen line. TIAN TIAN sits, her legs splayed forward, on a short pile of wood shavings, looking out, idly cleaning her teeth with a length of stick. This continues for a long moment.

PO: Still?

TIAN TIAN: Yeah.

PO: Every day. What do you think they want?

   (She shrugs, still picking her teeth.)

They just stand there and watch.

TIAN TIAN: Some of them wave their arms. The smaller ones.

PO: Yeah.

TIAN TIAN: Seems like they like us.

PO: It's hard to say.

TIAN TIAN: Maybe they do.

PO: But then they just go. And more come. Why?

TIAN TIAN: Why are you pacing?

PO: They make me restless.

TIAN TIAN: Come and sit down.

PO: I'm restless. Sometimes.

TIAN TIAN: I worry how it makes you look.

PO: What are you talking about?

TIAN TIAN: The relentless pacing. Back and forth. They'll think you're primitive.

PO: You ever wonder what they're saying?

(TIAN TIAN pats the ground next to her.)

TIAN TIAN : Sit with me, Po.

(He does. They sit side by side, looking out, his legs splayed forward like hers.)

PO: I wonder what they're saying sometimes. I watch their mouths move.

TIAN TIAN: It's a language, probably.

(He begins to play with some of the wood shavings, slowly and carefully scooping up a large handful in his cupped hands and dumping them over his head.)

PO: Their mouths opening and closing, their faces doing things. What do they want?

(He dumps more shavings over his head. She points out with her stick.)

TIAN TIAN: Like *that* one. Lots of face things.

(He dumps a load of shavings over her head too.)

PO: Do you think they're unhappy out there? That they need help?

TIAN TIAN: It's hard to say.

(He dumps another load of shavings over her head.)

PO: I feel like I should say something to that one. To all of them. Vocalize something.

TIAN TIAN: What would you say?

(She puts down her stick, beginning to groom him a bit, picking off the wood shavings from his hair and clothing, ignoring those on herself.)

PO: I don't know exactly. Something important about the world. Something they'd *need*.

TIAN TIAN: We speak different languages. There's no point.

PO: In the face of what's so hard. Or despair.

(*She continues her woodchip grooming. There is a slight pause.*)

PO: That feels good.

(*She continues grooming. He shakes himself vigorously, languorous with pleasure.*)

TIAN TIAN: Restlessness gone.

PO: *That's* what I'd say.

TIAN TIAN: *Ha.*

PO: The smell of these woodchips. Sharp. And sweet. Like the apples we had once . . . or the *pumpkin*. A thing crisp and tangy that comes out of the air in the sky and into your nose. Or how clean they make me. Refreshed and bright again. And then how good it feels when you are cared for by someone. Hands combing through your fur. Care and grooming. Your fingertips, Tian Tian. The attention of another being who is like you and *not*. *That* kind of clean. Do you think they know that?

TIAN TIAN : I don't know.

PO: They stare at us all the time but I don't think they do. They still don't know that your favorite scent is cinnamon and mine is mint. How I get restless and you stay put. But that we sit together like this in the woodchips. *That*, Tian Tian. Why else would we have come such a great way except to tell them? You from the far Exotic and me from—

TIAN TIAN: You aren't from a great way—

PO: But my *mother* from Exotic—

TIAN TIAN: A local boy, you are. Born right from *here* in the—

PO: My ancestry, I mean. My ancestry.

TIAN TIAN: They brought me to you from someplace far. One morning I was in a forest of bamboo in a Great Province and then suddenly I was in the sky tumbling and roaring and then—

PO: And then me.

TIAN TIAN: Yes. And then Po. Eventually.

(He dumps another handful of wood chips over her head.)

PO: Eventually.

(There is a slight pause.)

What I would *say* to them, Tian Tian.

TIAN TIAN: Okay, Po.

PO: *That.* How it would be better for them. The world. If.

TIAN TIAN: Okay.

(There is a pause. They look out.)

PO: How would I tell them?

TIAN TIAN: Esperanto.

PO: What?

TIAN TIAN: You just have to learn.

PO: (*Softly.*) Esperanto.

TIAN TIAN: You don't know what it is, do you?

PO: I'm only from *here.*

TIAN TIAN: When you travel like I have, you pick things up. *Mi iras en la domon*: I go into the house. *La birdo flugis en la arbon*: the bird flew into the tree. Esperanto.

PO: Oh.

TIAN TIAN: The grammar is easy: there are only sixteen basic rules, with no exceptions. You could learn.

PO: Yeah.

TIAN TIAN: No indefinite article, only definite ones. Nouns have the end "o" . . . to make the plural add the ending "j" . . . Adjectives end in "a" . . . Numbers *unu, du, tri, kvar, kvin, ses, sep, ok, naŭ, dek, cent, mil.*

PO: It sounds hard

TIAN TIAN: In 1873 Ludwik Zamenhof created it as a counterweight to national languages, which he believed divided people and were a source of conflict. If economic, ethnic, or religious differences divide people, Esperanto has the goal of uniting, allowing everyone who speaks different native languages to communicate, yet at the same time retain their own languages and cultural identities. The second major reason for Esperanto's success is that it's neutral. It belongs to no one. *Linguistic equality, Po.* Every person who uses Esperanto is on an equal linguistic footing with all other Esperantists. This promotes a spirit of connection and unity.

PO: Esperantists.

TIAN TIAN: *De kie vi estas?* Where are you from? *Ni iru spekti filmon.* Let's go to the movies. *Cu mi povas parole kun Maria?* Can I speak to Maria?

PO: Wow. Who is Maria?

TIAN TIAN: That's it. All I know.

   (There is a slight pause.)

PO: Do you sometimes wish they had never taken you here? Do you remember your life in the Great Province of Bamboo, before you ever smelled the smell of cinnamon or knew I was here?

TIAN TIAN: Oh. Do you know what we are in Esperanto, Po

PO: No.

TIAN TIAN: *Granda pando.*

PO: What's it mean?

TIAN TIA: It means us.

PO: Oh.

TIAN TIAN: And they are *uloj.* Folks.

PO: *Folks.* I knew they were something.

TIAN TIAN: No, I don't wish they had never taken me. Even if sometimes I do.

PO: Okay.

TIAN TIAN: *That's* what I would tell them. If I could.

(He begins picking woodchips from her clothing, grooming.)

PO: Someone could die, or stop loving you, or you could get sick. But if you look out of your house and they see *granda pando*, how bad could it be?

TIAN TIAN: That feels good.

(He grooms some more.)

PO: We can learn Esperanto. And teach them.

TIAN TIAN: I'd like that.

PO: For linguistic equality.

(There is a slight pause.)

TIAN TIAN: I love you.

PO: How do you say that in Esperanto?

TIAN TIAN: I'm not sure. But we can make it up. And then we'll translate.

PO: Okay.

TIAN TIAN: *Mi amas vin.*

PO: What's it mean?

TIAN TIAN: You try first. Say something.

PO: *Esti enamiginta kum.*

TIAN TIAN : Nice.

PO: Then we translate.

TIAN TIAN: I love you like an Elvis impersonator's love child loves the real Elvis.

PO: I love you like a chainsaw . . . or a sailboat.

TIAN TIAN: I love you like molasses poured over a mound of salt.

PO: I love you as if we'd never met.

TIAN TIAN: I love you as if we were kites flown in breezes too soft to feel.

PO: I could love you like a walking trail.

TIAN TIAN: I could love *you* like the last glass of water in a group mirage.

PO: If I didn't love you I'd be twelve feet tall and wear tight shoes and stick my fingers in people's plates in restaurants.

TIAN TIAN: If I didn't love *you* I'd wait in any waiting room I could find—in all waiting rooms in the world—and read their magazines, even if the languages were strange.

PO: I want you to love me like an old man's mustache drooping in a driving rainstorm.

TIAN TIAN: I want to be loved like a jerry-rigged machine, hulling walnuts and spitting out the shells.

PO: Can you do this? This love?

TIAN TIAN: Can *you*?

PO: This is how we say it. This is how. This.

(There is a long pause. They sit together on the woodchips. Legs splayed. Looking out. Together. Lights fade to black.)

EVERYBODY HITS

by Bruce Graham

Premiered May 18, 2018
Mile Square Theatre
7th Inning Stretch: Seven Ten-Minute Plays About Baseball
Hoboken, NJ
Artistic Director, Chris O'Connor

Director, Janice L. Goldberg

PHIL, Gene Santarelli
TED, Christian Castro
ASHLEIGH, Rebecca Muller

CHARACTERS

TED, 20s, Ashleigh's assistant.
PHIL, 60s, a baseball fan.
ASHLEIGH, 30s, a marketing exec.

SETTING

A Superbox at Citizen's Bank Park, Philadelphia.

TIME

Opening day. The present.

A super box. The window overlooking the field is the Fourth Wall. ASHLEIGH and TED, both young and sharply dressed, are in the process of showing PHIL the amenities. Everything PHIL wears has some sort of PHILLIES logo on it.)

TED: Not bad, huh? Right on third base. Clear view—no obstructions.

PHIL: (*Unimpressed.*) Uh-huh.

TED: Complimentary binoculars. Private bathroom, of course. Confidentially, it has a very strong exhaust fan so if you wanted to sneak a cigarette it's no big deal.

PHIL: Don't smoke.

TED: VIP parking.

PHIL: Don't drive.

TED: Remote control leather seating. Your own high-def TV for replays.

PHIL: This window open?

TED: Uhh, no.

ASHLEIGH: This is a private box owned by the team, Phil. It's our most exclusive.

PHIL: Yeah, ya keep sayin' that—

AHLEIGH: As I said, it's private, but, on rare occasions, you may have to share it with some VIPS.

TED: You could be sitting next to the mayor.

PHIL: Don't like the mayor.

ASHLEIGH It's okay. He hates baseball.

TED: Opening day, bang, gone by the third inning.

PHIL: And this window doesn't open, right?

TED: You have your own concierge. You want a beer you pick up this phone and a young lady brings it to you.

PHIL: Then I'd have to tip.

ASHLEIGH: Yes, but there's no line.

TED: How about that, huh Phil. No line.

PHIL: You think I'm payin' eight-fifty for a beer? See what I do is get a paper coffee cup with a lid—fill it fulla' vodka—and drink it on the subway here. I'm drunk till like the 6th inning and I save a fortune.

ASHLEIGH: That's very . . . creative.

TED: As a super box ticket holder you're also eligible to receive a ten percent discount on all merchandise.

ASHLEIGH: And—this is the best part—it's not just good for baseball games. This seat is yours for concerts. Springsteen, Billy Joel—

PHIL: So these widows don't open, that's what you're sayin'?

TED: That's the beauty of this, Phil. We're kind of hermetically sealed up here. Total climate control. When it's a hundred degrees with high humidity out there it's nice and comfortable in here.

ASHLEIGH: And here's the best part: Those people out there will be sooooo jealous. They all look up, sweating like maniacs, envying you the whole time, wishing they were up here—and they're not. They're not, Phil. But you are. You look down on them. It's a great feeling.

TED: So what do you think, Phil? Interested?

ASHLEIGH: Pretty sweet deal. There's a waiting list a mile long for this seat.

PHIL: Yeah, but the window—

ASHLEIGH: Will you forget the damned window?!! (*Silence.*) Sorry . . . sorry . . .

PHIL: You're not a baseball person, are you?

ASHLEIGH: Marketing.

TED: She came up with the Velcro umpire giveaway. You don't like a call you can take that little umpire and rip him apart.

PHIL: Hate that crap. Bobbleheads. Mascots. The big TV in center field. Nobody watches the damn game anymore.

(Silence.)

ASHLEIGH: Okay, so . . . well, as far as we can see—the biggest stumbling block here is . . . the window.

PHIL: 'Cause it doesn't open.

TED: Right.

PHIL: How're people gonna' hear me?

ASHLEIGH: Well, Phil—

PHIL: WOO-HOO, EVERYBODY HITS!

(His volume is amazing. TED and ASHLEIGH react as if someone blew an air horn right next to their ears.)

That's me, ya know. I'm the guy does that.

ASHLEIGH: Yes, Phil. We're aware of that.

PHIL: With that glass there nobody's gonna' hear me.

TED: That's kind of why we're here today, Phil—

PHIL: I been in that same seat four years now. WOO-HOO, EVERYBODY HITS! People love it.

ASHLEIGH: Actually, they don't.

PHIL: Hey, I know everybody in that section and they—

TED: We're not talking about in the actual ballpark, Phil.

ASHLEIGH: Your seat is right behind home plate. So that when you do your . . . catch-phrase—

PHIL: WOO-HOO, EVERYBODY HITS!

(Silence.)

ASHLEIGH: Yes, that one. Because of where your seat is located that goes out over radio and television.

PHIL: I'm a celebrity. Phil-the-fan. You should have a bobble-head day for me. Push down on the top and it yells, "WOO-HOO, EVERYBODY HITS!"

ASHLEIGH: (*Plowing on.*) The problem is, Phil, that you do it every time a batter comes to the plate. Every time. Ted, what are the numbers?

TED: An average nine-inning baseball game has 34.27 at bats. Multiply that by eighty-one home games and we're looking at 2,775.87 at bats a season.

ASHLEIGH: That means 2,775.87 times a season our audience has to hear—

(*Before Phil can . . .*)

Don't do it. Please.

TED: And our affiliates have been getting some complaints about it.

ASHLEIGH: Now, we're not trying to stifle your First Amendment rights here, Phil. It's not as if you're shouting profanities or hate speech it's just—well between the constant repletion and your . . . incredible volume it's become a little . . .

(*She looks for the right word.*)

TED: Obnoxious.

ASHLEIGH: I was going to say "problematic." That is why we are offering you—free of charge—this super box for the season. You're happy, the affiliates are happy—

PHIL: Who said I'm happy?

ASHLEIGH: Look at all this, Phil. It's yours for the season.

PHIL: What about next season?

ASHLEIGH: We can discuss that in the fall.

PHIL: Hey, just'cause I ride subways that don't mean I'm stupid. Sure, ya gimme this for a year and next year ya don't. Inna' meantime I lose my seat behind home plate. When I go to buy another one they'll be all sold out and I'll get stuck in center field. No thanks. (*Heading out.*)

ASHLEIGH: Two years! Guaranteed.

PHIL: What about a new window? One that opens? Then maybe I could bring in a bullhorn and lean out—

ASHLEIGH: We are not putting in a new window!

PHIL: That way they could hear me—

ASHLEIGH: Nobody wants to hear you! And besides, what you're saying is not true. Ted, gimme the numbers.

TED: Last year the team batting average was .228.

ASHLEIGH: So you see: everybody DOESN'T hit. What you're saying is basically a lie.

PHIL: I'm motivatin'.

ASHLEIGH: Motivatin'?

PHIL: The players love it.

ASHLEIGH: Oh please, Phil. You came here on the subway—they could buy the subway! The players don't give a rat's ass about people like you.

PHIL: Gonzalez thanked me every time. Said it inspired him.

TED: Gonzalez hit .130. He's down in Double A.

PHIL: He'll be back.

ASHLEIGH: Phil, look around. Look at this box. Be honest, did you ever sit down there, look up here, and wonder what it's like to sit up here?

PHIL: Not really.

ASHLEIGH: This is yours, Phil. Free of charge for two—no, three seasons. Three. I'll put it in writing.

PHIL: No thanks.

ASHLEIGH: Give us something to work with. What is it that you want, Phil?

PHIL: Go back to my seat and watch the game.

ASHLEIGH: This is the best seat in the stadium!

PHIL: It's not a "seat." It's a room. I could do this at home.

ASHLEIGH: What's the difference?

PHIL: Big difference.

ASHLEIGH: No there's not! What is your problem? Come on, please, tell me, what is missing from your life that you have to be out there every game—every goddamned game!—and yell like a . . . like a . . .

TED: Moron?

ASHLEIGH: Ted, stay out of this. Why, Phil? What compels you to . . . do this? Day after day, game after game—

PHIL: Why shouldn't I? It's America's past time.

ASHLEIGH: Oh, please. That's Netflix.

PHIL: Okay, I know this is somethin' you don't understand here, Ashleigh, but I love baseball. I just love it.

ASHLEIGH: How-can-you-love-it? It's boring! Ted, average time of a game?

TED: Three hours, five minutes, fourteen seconds.

ASHLEIGH: Out of which there's like five minutes of action.

PHIL: That's the beauty. Who need action alla' time? When I was a little kid and my parents made me go ta bed I'd take out my transistor radio and put it on the pillow there and just drift off listenin' to the game. Better'n a lullaby. And this box here, okay, it's nice I guess. I grew up in the cheap seats—before they even had these things. When I was a kid I'd come to the game with a bagga' baloney sandwiches and buy a program for a quarter. They'd give ya this stubby little pencil and I'd keep score. Every play. I wasn't there to talk on the phone or take pictures of myself, I was there to watch the game. No mascots or fireworks—the game. Just—the game. Lemmie tell ya somethin'—when the season ends I pick up a second job out on a loadin' dock. No wife, no kids, no car. My apartment is smaller than this box here. Why? So I can afford that seat out there. Eighty-one games a year—I'm out there. Rain delay—no problem. Extra innings? I love 'em.

    (Heading out.)

So, uhh, thanks but no thanks. I'm happy out there.

    (Reaches the door, turns back.)

WOO-HOO! EVERYBODY HITS!

(He exits. They stand there a moment. In the background we hear the beginning of the national anthem. Finally.)

ASHLEIGH: I will never understand these people . . .

(The lights fade.)

GREAT ESCAPES

by David Susman

Produced by
Actors Studio of Newburyport
Boston Theater Marathon XX
Artistic Director, Kate Snodgrass
May 6, 2018

Director, Tim Diering

LORRAINE, Kari Cretella-Nickou
FRED, Jim Manclark

CHARACTERS

FRED, Forties or fifties.
LORRAINE, Fred's mother; in her seventies or eighties.

SETTING

Fred's house.

TIME

Evening. The present.

FRED's *house; evening. An empty living room, not particularly stylish or ornate. The doorbell rings. After a beat, it rings again . . . several times, with urgency. FRED enters from the bedroom.*

FRED: Okay, okay . . .

> (*When he opens the door, LORRAINE bursts in. She uses a walker and clearly has limited mobility, but she moves with surprising speed and buzzes with energy.*)

LORRAINE: Thank God you're here! I was afraid I was going to have to hide in the bushes until you got home!

FRED: (*Amazed to see her.*) Jesus! Mom, what are you—?

LORRAINE: Close the door! They're probably out there right now, looking for me.

FRED: Who?

LORRAINE: Don't think they won't come after me, either. Ohhhh, they'll be plenty mad when they figure it out!

FRED: Who's looking—? Is everything all right? Mom, how did you even get here?

LORRAINE: By the skin of my teeth, that's how! Two taxis, three different buses . . . you have to keep switching, to make sure you're not being followed . . . Close the door, Fred! . . . Do you want me to get caught?

FRED: (*Closing the door.*) I don't understand . . . what's going on? Caught by who?

LORRAINE: Them. You think they'll sit idly by while one of their inmates has escaped? Believe me, they'll be out in full force, scouring the streets.

FRED: Mom, I don't know what you're talking about, but you shouldn't be riding the bus by yourself, especially at this time of night. Or taking taxis. I mean, with your hip, just getting in and out of them—. (*Beat.*) What do you mean, "escaped"?

LORRAINE: Escaped. Busted out. Made a break for it. Liberated myself from that gulag you and your brother put me in.

FRED: Shady Meadows isn't a gulag, Mom. It's an assisted-living facility, and a very nice one. Are you saying you left without telling anyone?

LORRAINE: Tell anyone? It was all I could do to avoid detection. There were some close calls, but so far I've managed to stay one step ahead.

FRED: Christ! You know you're not supposed to leave the grounds without notifying them. They must be worried sick!

LORRAINE: The only thing they're worried about is recapturing me. But that's not going to happen. See, I've got it all worked out. I'll lay low for a few hours, then after dark I'll make my way to the train station. It's safer than the airport. Now, they'll be expecting me to head south, to Mexico . . . so I'll head north, to Canada.

FRED: Are you nuts?! You can't go to Canada.

LORRAINE: Not to live, obviously. Just to throw the authorities off my trail. I'll hide out there until the heat is off, then I'll cross back into the States and work my way to the Rockies. I'll lay low in your brother's ski cabin until I can figure out my next move.

FRED: Mom, I don't know what's gotten into you, but you can't go traipsing all over North America. And you can't leave Shady Meadows without telling them! They were very explicit about that when we moved you in, remember? No leaving the building unaccompanied. It's for your own safety. You could be in a lot of trouble for this. They could evict you and we could lose our entire deposit.

LORRAINE: You seem stressed. Did I come at a bad time? Were you and Samantha in the middle of something?

FRED: Samantha's not here, Mom. And no, you didn't . . . I just don't understand what's going on. Why in the world would you want to leave Shady Meadows?

LORRAINE: To taste freedom, Fred! To throw off the shackles of oppression and feel the wind in my hair!

FRED: What oppression? Shady Meadows is perfectly nice. Beautiful grounds, kind staff, all sorts of activities.

LORRAINE: Are you kidding? The place is a prison. Eat when they tell you, sleep when they tell you, play games when they tell you. It's a penal colony!

FRED: Penal colonies don't have canasta, Mom.

LORRAINE: They thought they could tame me, break my spirit. But they underestimated me . . . that was their big mistake.

FRED: No one's trying to break your spirit. A few rules, that's all. No cooking in the rooms. No loud music after ten. No leaving the building without checking out at the front—. (*Beat.*) Wait a minute. How did you get past the front desk? Isn't there supposed to be an attendant there at all times?

LORRAINE: You mean Burt the Jailkeeper? He was there, all right. Believe me, it took plenty of planning to figure out a way around him.

FRED: I don't understand . . . you snuck past the attendant?

LORRAINE: Well, I hardly had to sneak. He was distracted by all the smoke.

FRED: What smoke?

LORRAINE: From the fire.

FRED: What fire?!

LORRAINE: The one in the television lounge. It's a classic diversionary technique. Ever read *The Art of War* by Sun Tzu?

FRED: You started a big fire?!

LORRAINE: Of course not. Do you think I'm a maniac? Of course I didn't start a big fire. (*Beat.*) I started a small fire.

FRED: Jesus Christ! Was anyone hurt?

LORRAINE: Don't be ridiculous . . . it was a controlled burn. I knew the lounge would be empty that time of night, so I just gathered some Popsicle sticks from the crafts room, added a few pine cones and a little rolled-up newspaper, and lit it in that hideous ceramic urn they keep in there.

FRED: Mom, someone could have been killed!

LORRAINE: Oh, please . . . I've seen bigger flames on a plate of fajitas. But the smoke, that was the real intimidation factor. The trick there is, I added some of Eunice's hair spray. The chemicals darken up the smoke, make it look like a real inferno.

FRED: Your roommate was in on this?

LORRAINE: Well, she was more of what you'd call an unknowing participant. I knew she'd never approve, so I waited until she was asleep, then I helped myself to her toiletries and stole into the night.

FRED: But you always said she was such a light sleeper.

LORRAINE: She is, generally. But tonight there may have been a little extra sedative in her orange juice.

FRED: You drugged Mrs. McClusky?!

LORRAINE: No, I didn't drug her. Am I crazy? I don't go around drugging my friends. (*Beat.*) I drugged her a little bit.

FRED: Mom! Do you have any idea how dangerous that it?

LORRAINE: Trust me, she's fine. She's getting the best night's sleep she's had in years. I gave her the good stuff . . . took it right from Doctor Adelman's private stash.

FRED: You stole drugs from the medical office?!

LORRAINE: Well, they practically leave the cabinet wide open. It only took a few minutes to pick the lock with a toothbrush and a bobby pin.

FRED: This is insanity! You can't go around wreaking havoc. And you can't leave Shady Meadows. It took a lot of work to find a place that you'd be comfortable and safe, and all you had to do was . . . was . . . be normal. Make friends . . . enjoy some quiet pastimes . . . not run around waging guerilla warfare!

LORRAINE: You're awfully tense. Are you sure I didn't interrupt something? Maybe you and Samantha were having relations?

FRED: No, Mom, we weren't—

LORRAINE: Because I know how frustrating it can be when you're in the middle of coitus, and you have to stop and—

FRED: We weren't—. Samantha doesn't live here anymore, Mom. We split up, remember?

LORRAINE: Of course I remember. I just thought she might still be coming by for the occasional playtime. Women have needs, you know.

FRED: Can we just get back to—?

LORRAINE: Especially that one. She may have been a little quiet, but underneath I could tell she was a hotsy-totsy. It's a shame you couldn't hold on to her.

FRED: (*Wearily.*) Yes, I know.

LORRAINE: Was it the money? Is that why she left? Because I always said, if you just asserted yourself at work a little more, that boss of yours would stop passing you over.

FRED: It wasn't money.

LORRAINE: (*Looking FRED up and down contemplatively.*) Maybe the way you dress. You've always been a little drab-looking, dear. You know, ladies like a man with some panache.

FRED: That's not why she left. I don't know why she left. She just said, "I need something else" and moved out.

LORRAINE: Well, did you ask what the something else was?

FRED: She didn't take follow-up questions. I got home, her things were packed, and she was halfway out the door. That was it. "I need something else."

LORRAINE: It's a pity, is all. You've always had such a difficult time with women. Now, your brother, he has to fight 'em off with a stick. A new one every week, it seems. Real lookers, too. Of course, women go for adventurous men like Hank. Skiing, rock climbing, skydiving . . . roaming from town to town, wherever the wind takes him. That's some life he leads!

FRED: (*Unenthusiastically.*) He's quite a fellow, yes.

LORRAINE: Maybe he could give you a few pointers. About women. I could ask him when I see him.

FRED: I don't need any advice from Tarzan, thank you. And you can't go trekking into the Rockies to find him.

LORRAINE: Of course I can. You think I don't know how to use a compass?

FRED: Mom, you have a bad hip . . . you have arthritis and neuropathy . . . you take five different medications before breakfast. You need care. And despite what you've been telling yourself, Shady Meadows is not Shawshank Prison. It's a pleasant and clean and well-run facility . . . assuming it's still standing.

LORRAINE: If you think it's so wonderful, why don't you go live there?

FRED: I would if I could. At least I'd be a well-behaved resident.

LORRAINE: You're a well-behaved everything, Fred. That's your problem. You're a rule follower. You always have been. You're diligent, polite, considerate. You don't cheat on your taxes. You drive the speed limit. You eat sensibly. You don't curse or chase women or embezzle money or get arrested for drunken disorderliness.

FRED: How ashamed of me you must be.

LORRAINE: I'm just saying, a little misbehavior would do you good.

FRED: We can't all be lunatics, Mom. We can't all go around setting fires and drugging our friends. Someone has to be responsible. Someone has to hold it all together.

LORRAINE: And where has it gotten you? Tell me that, Fred. What has all that good behavior done for you?

FRED: What's it done for me? I'll tell you what it's done for me: nothing! It's gotten me nowhere! I have no girlfriend and no money. I have a lousy job and an ungrateful boss. You think I don't want to be wild and cause trouble? You think I don't want to buck the system? Well, I can't. I have obligations. Shady Meadows costs money. You know where it comes from? The lousy job with the ungrateful boss! And who found you Shady Meadows in the first place? Who does everything for you, while Hank is off playing Hugh Hefner on ice? Me! Always me, Mom. While everyone else is having adventures and breaking away and escaping to new, wonderful lives, I'm just here. Where's my great escape, Mom? When do I get to break away?

LORRAINE: I didn't know you wanted to.

FRED: Well, I do. This isn't the life I was supposed to have. This isn't who I was supposed to be.

LORRAINE: Then be someone else.

FRED: I don't know how. I'm not like you and Hank and Samantha. I'm just . . . Fred. I'm drably dressed, underpaid, unadventurous Fred. (*Beat.*) How do you do it? How do you be . . . the way you are? Breaking the rules. Rebelling against everything. Taking all those risks.

LORRAINE: I had no choice. You and your brother stuck me in the Black Hole of Calcutta.

   (*Beat; off FRED's look.*)

I got old, Fred. When you get old, you run out of options. Everything becomes boring and safe. You realize the only excitement you'll ever have is if you make it yourself. The world isn't interested in making it for you. Not anymore. You want my advice? Don't get old. I hope you never do, Fred.

FRED: I already feel old.

LORRAINE: You're not. You don't have to be. You can change. You can be a whole different Fred, if that's what you want. Don't change too much, though. I like my Fred. He's kind and decent. He has a good heart. The world needs that. I need that. Even if I don't always say thank you. (*Beat.*) I have to go back to Shady Meadows, don't I?

FRED: Is it that bad?

LORRAINE: No. That's the problem.

   (*FRED grabs his jacket, keys.*)

FRED: Come on. I'll drive you. We'll smooth things over with the management.

   (*They start to exit, FRED helping LORRAINE along.*)

LORRAINE: You know, Eunice has a daughter. Divorced. I met her once. A terrible dresser, just like you. You two might hit it off.

FRED: We'll see, Mom. We'll take it one step at a time.

LORRAINE: She's not ready to date either. But in case you want it, I have her phone number.

FRED: Why did Mrs. McClusky give it to you, if she's not ready to date?

LORRAINE: Well, she didn't exactly give it to me . . .

   (*They exit.*)

HOT GECKO SPACE LOVE ACTION
(Based on a True Story)
by James McLindon

Originally produced by
Sandwich Arts Alliance, MA

Director, June Bowser-Barrett
Stage Manager, Rick Sharp

KENNETH, Bill Halloran
COOPER, Karen MacPherson
MISHA, Bud Hammond

CHARACTERS

COOPER, a female gecko, 18-35.
KENNETH, a male gecko, about the same age as Cooper.
MISHA, a Russian space fight supervisor, male or female, any age.

Race-blind and diverse casting is encouraged.

SETTING

An aging Russian spacecraft that has seen better days.

The Russian National Anthem plays. Two post-coital geckos, KENNETH, *a male, and* COOPER, *a female, are breathing hard, splayed out on the wall. For several seconds they are still. One, then the other, shoots out her tongue and wiggles it, then withdraws it quickly.*

COOPER: Oh, Kenneth . . . that was amazing!

KENNETH: God, it so was.

COOPER: That thing you did with your tongue. Holy crap.

KENNETH: Not to brag, but it helps to have one as long as your forearm.

COOPER: Was it okay for you? I mean, you weren't bored or anything?

KENNETH: Bored?

COOPER: No, it's just in the middle, you stopped. It looked like you were . . . licking your eyes. Look I know I can take a while—

KENNETH: Oh, god, no, I wasn't bored. I just . . . don't have any eyelids.

COOPER: Oh. Oh!

KENNETH: You're lucky, most geckos don't. After a while, I gotta lick them or they dry out and everything's all blurry.

COOPER: *That's* what's hot about you! No eyelids makes you look so . . . intense. I hate my lids.

KENNETH: I love 'em. They make you look so mysterious. Like, one second, your eyes are there and then, poof: they're gone!

(They're becoming aroused. Staying stuck to the wall, they approach each other. Very close. A pause. Then their tongues flick all around. It's not necessary that the actors actually lick each other. But the illusion should be that they are and that it is how geckos kiss. When they finish, both are very aroused.)

KENNETH: Wow, I've never let a girl lick my eyes before. God, let's do it again.

(MISHA is never seen. Rather, s/he is only a voice with a heavy Russian accent. A dry, defeated voice.)

MISHA: *Nyet*! No make-loving for twelve more minutes. *Spasibo.**

COOPER: Oh, c'mon, Misha!

MISHA: Is deal. You get free ride Russian spaceship, we get study effects weightlessness on gecko mating, and you follow strict protocol—

(*Suddenly, the space ship jolts, the lights flicker.*)

KENNETH: Oh my god! Misha. What was that!? (*Long pause.*) Misha!?

MISHA: Mmmmm, is nothing. Is not to worry.

COOPER: (*Whispering to* KENNETH.) I told you we shouldn't go with a Russian mission!

KENNETH: It wasn't nothing. Tell us what's happening.

MISHA: Mmmm, issss . . . a little to worry.

COOPER: What is?

MISHA You know how Korolyov is our Mission Control, our Houston, da?

KENNETH: Yeah.

MISHA: "Korolyov, we have a problem." (*Pause: no response.*) Ha, ha. Is good Tom Hanks joke, no? I've been saving it.

KENNETH: How big a problem?

MISHA: Is not to worry.

COOPER: How big a problem!? Is this rustbucket gonna fall apart?

MISHA: No, no, no. (*Pause.*) We have just, uhhhh, lost all communications with spacecraft computer.

COOPER: What!? Well . . . well . . . we can try to fix it from up here, right? Like Tom Hanks did?

MISHA: Tom Hanks had opposable thumbs, yes? You are sex geckos.

KENNETH: We are not *sex* geckos. We are geckos . . . who have chosen, in the interest of science, to go into space so . . . so . . .

---

* "Thank you."

MISHA: So Russians could observe, record your sex making.

KENNETH: So *scientists* could. Which makes us also, like, scientists. And we prefer to call it mating.

MISHA: Sex mating, da, whatever.

COOPER: So, are we about to die up here or what?

KENNETH: Cooper! We're not going to die up here. Right? Misha?

MISHA: Mmmm . . . no. (*Pause.*) Very unlikely.

COOPER: Oh my god, we should've gone American. Really, Misha?

MISHA: Mmmm, is maybe a little likely. In sense you are hurtling through void of space out of control.

COOPER/KENNETH: Holy God!/Are you kidding me!?

MISHA: Space ship hard to control. Is not like American president. Ha, ha, I make good joke lighten mood. Is not to worry.

COOPER: How is this not to worry?

MISHA: Video feed still crystal clear.

KENNETH: Wait, you guys're watching us live?

COOPER: We were told just authorized scientists would have access to recordings later.

MISHA: Engineers bored so I throw you up on big screen. First time you mated, all Korolyov Mission Control center burst into applause. Mission accomplished, yes!?

COOPER: You did what!

KENNETH: When you say, big screen, how big do you—

MISHA: Seventy-five-meter screen.

COOPER: Seventy— Oh my god.

MISHA: Samsung HD.

COOPER: Oh my god!

MISHA: Ultra HD 4k. Close-ups are amazing—

COOPER: Stop it!

KENNETH: Why do you all want to watch us have sex?

MISHA: Mmmm . . . Look. Is little bit scientific inquiry, little bit new Russian entrepreneurial spirit. Is very hard find new internet porn category, yes? All good ones taken. Most bad ones taken. We are thinking outside cube.

COOPER: Outside the box.

MISHA: Outside box, da. Lizard sex. No one has done this. This could be next big thing.

KENNETH: (*Interested.*) Really?

COOPER: Kenneth!

MISHA: Da. Although iguanas . . . . Very sexy reptile.

COOPER: Well, what about our tongues? They can't touch our tongues.

MISHA: Is true. Gecko tongue vibrator now biggest sexy toy in Moscow porn shops.

COOPER: Wait. Are we already on the Internet?

MISHA: No, no, no. (*Pause.*) Yes. Only beta testing. But . . . very strong numbers. Iguanas though. Ho, very massive tail.

KENNETH: Well . . . my tail's pretty massive.

   (*MISHA snorts.*)

It is!

MISHA: For porn, is a little . . . diminutive.

KENNETH: Diminu— Cooper, tell him. My tail is not diminutive . . .

COOPER: No, right, it's not, it's very . . . very . . . adequate.

KENNETH: Adequate!?

COOPER: Can we get back to how bad this is? Misha, if you can't control our spacecraft, why shouldn't we panic?

MISHA: You are in orbit. You will just stay there while we work.

COOPER: We're supposed to be home in six days. Will you have it fixed in six days?

MISHA: (*Calculating.*) Engineers about to leave for weekend. Monday is holiday. We start on Tuesday. (*Pause.*) Wednesday if engineers hungover,

KENNETH: We're supposed to be back on Wednesday. Like, do we have enough food if it's longer?

MISHA: Mmmm . . . Yes.

KENNETH: Misha!?

MISHA: No. You have two days' worth food.

COOPER: But we weren't supposed to be back for five more days.

MISHA: Focus groups prefer watch skinnier geckos for sex-making.

COOPER: What the hell is that supposed to mean!?

KENNETH: What will we eat!?

MISHA: Animal Planet say geckos opportunistic cannibals.

COOPER: We. Are. Not! Tell him, Kenneth, we would rather die than eat each other. (*Pause.*) Kenneth? Well, I would! I am not eating you!

   (*MISHA giggles.*)

Shut up, Misha! Any other part of your disaster we should know about?

MISHA: Mmmm . . . no. Yes. Is only . . . orbit degrade unless correction. We cannot now correct.

COOPER: So . . . we return to earth a little sooner?

MISHA: Mmmm . . . Yes. In uncontrolled atmospheric reentry. In which, spacecraft becomes giant . . . oh, what is English. Football? No. Foosball? No. Oo, fireball! You become giant fireball!

COOPER: Fireball!?

MISHA: Is not to worry. Engineers work on it, Wednesday latest. They will still have twelve hours to fix. Or eight. So! Next event begins three minutes. All engineering team is waiting before start weekend. And . . . we stream live pay-per-view.

COOPER: There's no research protocol, is there!? It's just your pay-per-view schedule! Is this really how I go? In a porn shoot on a crappy Russian spaceship desperately hoping a bunch of crappy, hungover Russians engineers save me while a crappy Russian flight supervisor lies to me! (*A long, deeply wounded pause.*) Hello?

(*Off KENNETH's glare.*)

Misha?

MISHA: You geckos. You are very hurtful reptiles. You have wounded engineers. You have wounded me. You have wounded Russia.

COOPER: We're hurtful!? You're about to kill us!

MISHA: You defeat old Soviet Union. So, we try be capitalists, so you like us better. But no. You say we meddle your elections, are bandit state, failed oligarchy where rich run everything.

COOPER: Well . . . y'know, if the shoe fits . . .

MISHA: America is oligarchy!

COOPER: No, we're not—

MISHA: Koch brothers. Mercer family. Donald Trump. If shoe fits . . .

COOPER: Okay, maybe a little.

MISHA: Russians have feeling, too, you know.

COOPER: I . . . I know. I'm sorry.

MISHA: We are just trying be good capitalist. Pay-per-view is robust revenue stream, yes?

KENNETH: I don't know. How many of our events have you streamed?

MISHA: Mmmm . . . some. (*Pause.*) Many. (*Pause.*) All.

COOPER: Jesus. Okay, you tell the engineers: No more "events" till you fix this spaceship.

MISHA: But we will have to refund pay-per-view!

COOPER: There'll be others. But only if you don't kill us. Tell them.

(*We hear MISHA say some words in Russian off-mike.*)

MISHA: Wounded engineers want sexy tease first, then save you.

COOPER: All right, we'll give them a tease. But we need a second.

MISHA: Fine.

(*Muttering.*)

Iguanas would never pull stunt like this.

COOPER: You really aren't sure if you would eat me? Cuz I thought we were both starting to feel . . . something.

KENNETH: Of course I wouldn't eat you. I meant, I would let you eat me, Cooper. Part of me. My tail.

MISHA: Animal Planet say gecko detach tail when predator attack.

COOPER: Misha, Please!

MISHA: I have intriguing thought about tail for next event—

COOPER/KENNETH: NO!

KENNETH: I'd gladly detach mine to save you. Unless you think it's too . . . diminutive.

COOPER: I don't. I think it's perfect.

(*They kiss.*)

MISHA: (*Teary.*) Was beautiful. All engineers weep at your love story. They will return to desks save you. Also, focus group say adding emotional content enhances porn experience.

COOPER/KENNETH: You let the focus group watch that!?

MISHA: No. (*Pause.*) Yes. Come, is sexy-tease time. All engineering team awaits. Please?

(*The GECKOS, angry, turn to each other. Slowly, they calm. KENNETH flicks his tongue. They become aroused.*)

COOPER/KENNETH: Da.

(*Their tongues explode, resuming their magic. The Russian National Anthem plays. Lights down slowly.*)

THE KITTY BOMB

by Kevin Daly

World premiere at the Acorn Theatre in Manhattan.

Produced by
New York New Works Festival
September 6–15, 2018
New York, NY

Festival Director and Producer, Gene Fisch Jr.

TOMMY, Keegan McDonald
DAVID, Johnnie Jackow
KATE, Mariette Straus

Director, Kim T. Sharp
Stage Manager, Collins Hilton

CHARACTERS

KATE BEECKER, 26, a kindergarten teacher. There's kindness, enthusiasm, and a touch of disorganization in everything she does.
DAVID BEECKER, 24. insurance salesman. KATE'S younger brother.
TOMMY BEECKER, 27, KATE'S older brother. He's taken stabs at many creative careers. Today he's an entrepreneur.

SETTING AND TIME

KATE'S living room. The present.

At rise. KATE'S living room.
The room feels warm and welcoming.
Three siblings are mid-discussion.

TOMMY is pitching his latest entrepreneurial idea.
KATE is being supportive.
DAVID, not so much.

TOMMY: People die all the time. It can happen suddenly without warning. Dave, I think of you and your family out for a drive, BOOM, car accident. You're all dead.

DAVID: OK, I'm done.

KATE: Wait a minute. Hear him out.

TOMMY: Can I ask you a question? What's going to happen to your cat?

DAVID: (*To Kate.*) Is he kidding me?

KATE: It's a legitimate question.

TOMMY: What's going to happen to the cat, Dave?

DAVID: (*To Kate.*) You want me to take this seriously?

KATE: I do.

DAVID: OK, if my family and I are in a car accident the last thing I'm worrying about is my cat.

KATE: That's his point.

TOMMY: Your cat's going to starve to death.

DAVID: Why wouldn't you feed it?

TOMMY: What if I'm in the car with you?

DAVID: Kate would feed the cat.

TOMMY: She's in the car too.

DAVID: I couldn't fit that many people.

TOMMY: Kate and I were driving in the car that hit you. We're all dead.

DAVID: What are the chances of that happening?

KATE: You have to use some imagination.

DAVID: We all die in a car accident?

TOMMY: What happens to the cat?

DAVID: My mother-in-law has a key.

TOMMY: What if she didn't?

DAVID: I would get her one.

TOMMY: I want you to imagine what that would be like for the cat.

DAVID: Being stuck with my mother-in-law?

KATE: David, be serious.

DAVID: Come on, Kate. This is funny.

TOMMY: You said five minutes. You couldn't even give me thirty seconds.

KATE: (*To Tommy.*) Finish the pitch. He'll listen.

TOMMY: He doesn't want to hear it.

KATE: (*Taking him aside.*) He does. He does. Tell it to him the way you told me. Take a moment. He'll listen.

TOMMY: OK.

KATE: You have something important to say.

> (*TOMMY reaches into a cardboard box lying on the floor and withdraws his invention: The Kitty Bomb.*)

DAVID: This is too much.

TOMMY: Can I ask you a question? Do people love their animals? And you're right—the chances of you, me, Kate, your kids, your wife, your in-laws all dying in a car crash are probably small.

DAVID: Probably.

TOMMY: But there's people who don't have families. They have cats. If those people die in car accidents what happens to their cats?

KATE: They starve.

TOMMY: That's why I invented the Kitty Bomb.

(Places the Kitty Bomb on the living room table.)

It's an explosive on a timer that you put in the cat food.

DAVID: Stop right there.

TOMMY: Every night when you feed your cat you set the timer back twenty-four hours. If something happens to you and you don't reset the timer it explodes emptying the bag of cat food so the cat can eat until someone comes to save them.

KATE: Let me get my checkbook.

DAVID: No. We're not putting money into this. Is that an explosive?

TOMMY: It's not turned on.

DAVID: You want to sell people a bomb?

KATE: *(Reassuringly.)* A small bomb.

TOMMY: It doesn't have to be cat food. Dog food. Bird food. I see a whole line of pet bombs.

DAVID: Pet bombs?

TOMMY: People would buy this.

DAVID: For revenge.

KATE: I would buy it.

DAVID: You don't have a cat.

(TOMMY prepares to take notes.)

TOMMY: Tell me what don't you like about it?

DAVID: The explosion.

TOMMY: It's not for people with children.

DAVID: Or people with cats.

TOMMY: You don't like this idea. I have others. Let me show you.

DAVID: Let's hold those for another time.

(*TOMMY exits.*)

DAVID: No, don't bother, I need to . . .

(*Turning to KATE.*)

I need to get home. I told Maureen I was leaving work half an hour ago. We have an event tonight.

KATE: Five more minutes. That's all.

DAVID: I need you to understand when I say I'm busy I'm actually busy.

(*Looks at his phone, frustrated.*)

I can stay five minutes—at most.

KATE: This is good for him. He needs our support.

DAVID: The Kitty Bomb?

KATE: A little optimism. A pinch of engagement. It would go a long way.

(*DAVID picks it up. Examines it.*)

DAVID: Am I safe holding this thing?

KATE: He worked hard on that you know. He was excited to share it with you.

DAVID: Don't give him money for this.

KATE: He went to a seminar. We should be supportive.

DAVID: They're going to put us on the No-Fly List.

(*DAVID puts the Kitty Bomb back in the cardboard box.*)

Tell me you're not worried about him.

KATE: Actually, I'm worried about my younger brother.

DAVID: You're worried about me?

KATE: You look stressed.

DAVID: I am stressed.

KATE: Work or home?

DAVID: It's my sister. She calls every day.

KATE: I have to call or I'd never see you.

DAVID: You really picked the worst day for this. I've got like a million emails I still need to return.

KATE: A million.

> *(TOMMY returns wearing a traditional Scottish kilt, a Highlander shirt, and a tam o' shanter cap.)*

TOMMY: Can I ask you a question?

DAVID: *(Seeing his brother's outfit.)* OK, now I'm done.

KATE: You have to hear the idea.

TOMMY: It's a party bus. I got the idea at your bachelor party. We rented a limo and drove to the casino. Do you remember that?

DAVID: I remember my bachelor party.

TOMMY: It wasn't fun.

DAVID: OK.

TOMMY: It was just you, me, and Kate's husband Marc. We're not really party people are we? But wasn't that night supposed to be fun? Didn't we want to have a good time?

DAVID: Now I'm really glad I came over.

TOMMY: Can I ask you a question? What would you pay for a party bus where in addition to the driver you also get a traditional Scottish party guide?

DAVID: Nothing. I would pay nothing.

TOMMY: You have the option to get an authentic Scottish party-guide with the kilt, bagpipes, and even one of these little hats they wear . . .

KATE: Tam o' shanter.

TOMMY: Or just a regular Scottish guy in jeans and a Highlander t-shirt. The point is this guy becomes your party guide. He drinks scotch. He has scars from bar fights. He sings folk songs. He knows when and how to talk to women. He makes you feel like a man. I'm calling it MacBuddies. Get it? Mac—

DAVID: I get it.

KATE: Let me get my checkbook.

DAVID: That's a terrible name. And even if it wasn't we're not Scottish. You don't know anything about being Scottish. It's going to end up a caricature, you're going to insult people.

KATE: Not necessarily.

TOMMY: People would pay for this.

(DAVID'S phone rings during the following. He looks at the phone and chooses to ignore the call. It happens once more before he finally picks up.)

DAVID: That's where you're going wrong Tommy—it's not about what people will pay for. It's about what people need. They don't need a Scottish party guide any more than a pipe bomb in their pantry. I hate to be the one to break it to you but these stupid get rich quick schemes are not real inventions. You're a college dropout who's spent the past ten years inventing ways to avoid the real world. Get a job. Do something with yourself. Do something meaningful with your life. And most importantly stop wasting my time. Both of you.

(Answers phone, it's his wife, his frustration carrying over.)

What? . . . I'm on my way . . . I was just about to . . . Yes, I know they do but I was just . . . If you'd let me . . .

(She hangs up.)

Great. Can't wait to get home.

(DAVID makes to exit.)

TOMMY: (*To Kate.*) Did you tell him?

KATE: Leave it alone.

DAVID: Tell me what?

KATE: It's nothing. You should go.

TOMMY: I thought the whole point was to do something together.

DAVID: What are you talking about?

KATE: (*Pause.*) Marc moved out this morning. He's been moved out for a while. He just took most of his things today.

(*DAVID looks around the room. Notices the missing things. Marc's things.*)

DAVID: Why didn't you say anything?

KATE: There's nothing to say.

(*DAVID sits down next to his sister. Processing it all. There's a lot he wants to say. A lot he wants to ask. Instead he says, to TOMMY.*)

DAVID: What else you got?

TOMMY: How do you feel about peanut butter that isn't made from peanuts?

DAVID: It's not peanut butter.

TOMMY: It's peanut butter for people who are allergic to peanuts.

DAVID: If they're allergic to peanuts why would you call it peanut butter?

(*The Kitty Bomb EXPLODES. We hear the ringing in their ears. They speak at each other. We don't hear it. They don't hear it. Only ringing.*)

(*DAVID is attempting to berate his brother. Large gestures. TOMMY is trying to figure out what went wrong.*)

(*KATE is laughing and crying and laughing.*)

LIVING HISTORY

by Brent Lewis

Production by
Cecil College Music and Theatre
November 2–3, 2018

Director, Kelly Bostic

AL CAPONE, Jessie Fitzgerald
BENJAMIN FRANKLIN, Dana Hoffman
MARK TWAIN, Kali Craig
ALBERT EINSTEIN, Morgan Terrell
WILBUR WRIGHT, Makenzie Wiegand
ORVILLE WRIGHT, Mary Poorman

CHARACTERS

BEN FRANKLIN, just a regular history reenactor doing a job.
AL CAPONE, a hammy middle-management type.
MARK TWAIN, a quote master.
ALBERT EINSTEIN, a hipster doofus.
WILBUR WRIGHT, the smart brother.
ORVILLE WRIGHT, the smartass brother.

Casting open to all ages.

SETTING

The employee breakroom at a living history museum during working hours.

A small employee breakroom. Typical office furnishings are onstage—a table, a couple of uncomfortable chairs, a coffee maker, and a microwave—but also some museum-specific items such as a mannequin wearing historical dress, a variety of famous hats, and various items of historical significance such as muskets, antiques, and early versions of the American flag. A prominent wall sign features a logo for the Museum of Living History; *a smaller, less elaborate font reads:* Employee Breakroom. *A door opens.* AL CAPONE, *sporting his famous pinstripe suit, fedora, boutonniere, and scarred face, enters. He holds the door for the others.*

CAPONE: Alright, palookas, take your break, enjoy a Coke and a smoke, but don't bother getting too comfy. You're back on the chain gang in ten minutes.

(In succession, dressed appropriately but shabbily, the following characters enter: BEN FRANKLIN—stout, bald wig, glasses, coat-and-britches; carrying a kite, MARK TWAIN—white hair, white moustache, white suit with white bowtie, WILBUR and ORVILLE WRIGHT, the first bald, the second dark haired and mustachioed, but nothing indicates who they might be, and ALBERT EINSTEIN—wild hair and moustache, pipe; simple mid-twentieth-century clothing.)

And remember: no real smoking. Of anything. I'm looking at you, Einstein. Don't make me call the coppers on ya.

EINSTEIN: (*Pulling off his wig and scratching his head vigorously.*) Man, this thing itches. Hey, Mr. Capone, can I *not* be Einstein tomorrow? It's my turn to play the F to the D to the R. Can I get a Delano up in here?

FRANKLIN: You just want to sit in the wheelchair all day.

CAPONE: And what happened the last time I gave you the chair, ya nincompoop?

EINSTEIN: I wasn't properly trained. I thought you said Roosevelt had narcolepsy.

TWAIN: All you need in life is ignorance and confidence, and then success is sure. That's what I, Mark Twain, always say.

EINSTEIN: Plus fighting Hitler is tiring. And the kids seemed to enjoy seeing how presidents need naps, too.

TWAIN: The public *is* the only critic whose opinion is worth anything at all.

FRANKLIN: *Those* kids wrote all over your face in permanent marker.

CAPONE: I have to admit, I did get a kick outta that. Okay, now listen up, chumps. As floor manager, I gotta take a powder to go palaver with the big cheese upstairs, see? We're lousy with school groups today. The little rubes are bum-rushing the joint. Cool your heels, and I'll be back in two shakes with your marching orders. Meanwhile, here's next week's schedule for you dirty rats to eyeball.

(He gives EINSTEIN the schedule and exits.)

FRANKLIN: Sheesh. He's like if James Cagney and ten pounds of cheese had a baby. Who's out on the floor now?

WILBUR WRIGHT: Babe Ruth, Frederick Douglass, Clara Barton, Marilyn Monroe, and Cochise.

FRANKLIN: Ugh. Cochise.

WILBUR WRIGHT: We have got to do something about Cochise, right? I don't feel right playing Cochise.

EINSTEIN: Oh! Shoot. You ain't gonna like this Benjy, my man.

(Handing the schedule to FRANKLIN, he recommences head scratching.)

FRANKLIN: Stop calling me Benjy. I've told you a hundred times, my name is—

(Glancing at schedule.)

Dang it!

EINSTEIN: Sorry, dang it.

WILBUR WRIGHT: What's the problem? My brother and I are good at solving problems.

FRANKLIN: Capone put me on the schedule for Saturday even though I told him not to.

TWAIN: When angry, count to four: when very angry, swear.

FRANKLIN: Could you chill out on the quotes for just one minute?

WILBUR WRIGHT: You've got to give him credit for commitment.

EINSTEIN: I think this wig gave me bugs.

(The door bursts open. CAPONE leans in holding a walkie-talkie.)

CAPONE: Listen up, pigeons. We've got us a fracas on the third floor. Elvis and Billy the Kid got into a shoving match, and Helen Keller just punched Elvis right in his lip curl. They might need us to fill in up there, so cool the baloney another coupla tick-tocks and I'll—

EINSTEIN: Helen Keller? She seems so nice. And quiet.

CAPONE: She's a real fine tomato, that Helen Keller, but I hear her and the King of Rock-n-Roll have been dancing the ol' hotsie-totsie, if ya know what I mean.

FRANKLIN: Hey, Al, you said I could have Saturday off for my cousin's wedding.

CAPONE: Say, are you trying to pull one over on me, Baldy? You know the rules. If you're on the schedule you work the schedule. A group of VIPs will be here on Saturday. It's all hands on deck. And no switching days, Kitestring. The rule is, no finagling with the schedule unless approved by a floor manager.

FRANKLIN: But you're our floor manager.

CAPONE: And I ain't signing it. I ain't never signed no shift swap, and I ain't never signing no shift swap. I didn't get to the level I'm at in this here swanky dustbin by just signing off for every reenactor who wanted to go on the lam. A man has to have his standards, Bifocals, and this man has a perfect record.

TWAIN: The less there is to justify a traditional custom, the harder it is to get rid of it.

FRANKLIN: Come on, Al. If I can get somebody to trade with me, sign off.

CAPONE: You can quit your gum-bumping, Franklin, and wipe that sour puss off your mug. Even if you find yourself a patsy willing to wear your Chicago overcoat for ya, I ain't signing nothing. No way. No how. The rules is the rules. Now hold on to your gumdrops youse boobs, I got a call coming in.

(*He exits.*)

EINSTEIN: That's a bummer. I could cover for you. I think everybody should spend as much time with their family as possible. I call that my Theory of Relatives.

WILBUR WRIGHT: You are so dumb, Einstein.

EINSTEIN: Yeah? Well, who the heck are you two even supposed to be?

WILBUR WRIGHT: You know that we're Wilbur and Orville Wright.

EINSTEIN: But who even knows what Orville and Wilbur Wright look like? Shouldn't you be wearing leather caps, like the one Snoopy wears?

WILBUR WRIGHT: For our era, we are appropriately dressed, am I not correct, brother Orville?

(*ORVILLE nods his head gleefully.*)

EINSTEIN: Yeah, well, maybe you should have invented a machine you could use to fly somewhere and buy yourselves a couple personalities, you airborne weirdos.

TWAIN: There it is; it doesn't make any difference who we are or what we are, there's always somebody to look down on.

FRANKLIN: My mom will be intolerable if I don't make it to Madeline's wedding.

EINSTEIN: Maybe you can trick Al into signing off.

ORVILLE WRIGHT: (*Holds up a mocking white paper moustache and quotes Twain.*) Many a small thing has been made large by the right kind of advertising.

FRANKLIN: That's good. Who said that?

ORVILLE WRIGHT: I think maybe it was one of the Kardashians.

(*TWAIN shoots ORVILLE a sideways hey-wait-a-minute look. The others nod with gullibility, and not without a hint of admiration for ORVILLE.*)

FRANKLIN: That's really not a bad idea.

(*CAPONE reenters.*)

CAPONE: Alright, mannequins. The hubbub is over. Elvis and Helen have kissed and made up. Turns out Billy the Kid was just keeping the peace.

FRANKLIN: Al. We have to talk about the schedule swap. Einstein here is willing to work for me on Saturday. He's got Benjamin Franklin down. He can do it.

EINSTEIN: We are all born ignorant, but one must work hard to remain stupid. Dude.

FRANKLIN: See? He's got this. You should sign off on the shift switch.

CAPONE: I should, should I? And why is that ya big galoot?

FRANKLIN: Look at it this way. Is there a better Capone than you in this whole place?

CAPONE: Not a chance, Lightning Bolt.

FRANKLIN: And you're the best Robert E. Lee that ever walked the floors of this museum.

CAPONE: I would say you're probably right about that, too.

TWAIN: We like a man to come right out and say what he thinks, as long as we agree.

FRANKLIN: And when you're John Brown. Man, when you're John Brown I feel like running off to Harper's Ferry to warn them you've returned.

CAPONE: Heh. Tell 'em old Oswatomie Brown is back in town, baby!

TWAIN: A man can live for two months on a good compliment.

ORVILLE WRIGHT: None but an ass pays a compliment and asks a favor at the same time.

TWAIN: Quit stealing my lines. Wilbur, make him stop. You're the smart one.

WILBUR WRIGHT: (*Raising a fake Mark Twain moustache identical to his brother's.*) Compliments embarrass me. I always feel that they haven't said enough.

TWAIN: Really? You're perpetuating this kind of theft of my intellectual property?

FRANKLIN: Al Capone. General Lee. John Brown. You always play the outlaw, the rebel, the resister. And there's nobody who works here that is better at it than you.

CAPONE: Go on, we all know I'm the bee's knees, but I'm listening.

FRANKLIN: But you also always follow the rules. To really feel the vibe, to really be your characters, shouldn't you *break* the rules? *Be* the rebel? *Resist*? At least once?

CAPONE: My perfect record though.

FRANKLIN: Come on, man, you don't play Cotton Mather or Andrew Carnegie.

CAPONE: I have built my organization upon fear.

FRANKLIN: Or J. Edgar Hoover.

CAPONE: (*With loathing and a shaking of his fist.*) Hoover.

FRANKLIN: I think it would notch your portrayals up into perfection. Come on Al, be the gangster you always knew you could be. Sign off on the shift switch.

CAPONE: You're right. About all of it.

FRANKLIN: Aw, man, you're the greatest, Al.

CAPONE: But I still ain't signing off. Now cut your chin music and get back to work.

(*He opens the breakroom door and the reenactors begin to file out, The WRIGHT BROTHERS, EINSTEIN and his wig, TWAIN, and then FRANKLIN.*)

FRANKLIN: (*On his way out.*) I'll give you twenty bucks.

CAPONE: I got more integrity than that, ya sap. Nothing less than twenty-five.

FRANKLIN: (*Pulling cash out of his britches.*) You know, some people would call this racketeering.

CAPONE: I call it a business. Now get out there and earn your paycheck, you dirty rat.

   (Blackout.)

THE MILK OF HUMAN KINDNESS

by J. Thalia Cunningham

Produced by
Rhino Theatre
Pompton Lakes, NJ
August 2018

ABDULLAH FAROOQ, David Colberg
ARIANA, Elizabeth Quiñones

Director, Mike Gogel

CHARACTERS

ABDULLAH FAROOQ, Mid-late 20s, looks older. Bearded. Polite, gracious, occasionally obsequious. Has Middle Eastern accent. Dressed in conservative American garb.

ARIANA, TSA security staff at JFK. Mid 20s-30s. Ernest. Takes her job and herself seriously but wants to be kind. Wears TSA uniform with name tag on pocket.

SETTING

JFK Airport. British Airways security check.

TIME

The present.

At rise: Table with plastic bins, for items going through x-ray screening. ABDULLAH enters carrying Styrofoam cooler (not too large.). Grabs plastic bin. Removes shoes, watch, belt, jacket. Empties pockets of keys, loose change and places them in bin. Sets cooler down alongside bin.

ARIANA: . . .please don't forget to empty *all* metal from your pockets.

(ABDULLAH re-checks his pockets. Slides cooler and plastic bin along table.)

What's in there?

ABDULLAH: The cooler? My wife's milk.

ARIANA: What do you mean, your wife's milk?

ABDULLAH: For the baby.

ARIANA: Baby? Where is it?

ABDULLAH: With his mother. And our other children.

ARIANA: Why aren't they traveling with you?

ABDULLAH: They left yesterday. To visit relatives . . . London. My wife's mother had a heart attack.

ARIANA: Why didn't you give her a break, take the kids, so she only had the baby to deal with?

ABDULLAH: She wanted them with her.

ARIANA: That milk isn't doing the baby much good if you're carrying it.

ABDULLAH: My wife got a respiratory infection. Her doctor said she needed antibiotics, but she's allergic to penicillin and most of the other antibiotics they use.

ARIANA: So? I needed antibiotics once after I had a baby.

ABDULLAH: The doctor gave her . . . uh . . . Tetracycline. Yes, that's it. The only antibiotic she's not allergic to that would help the infection.

ARIANA: It's okay to take antibiotics while you're breastfeeding.

ABDULLAH: Except for this one. Her doctor said Tetracycline stains a baby's teeth. It could stop his bones from growing. He could be deformed.

ARIANA: Oh, my God! Didn't she take formula with her? Why do you need this milk?

ABDULLAH: She stored this in the freezer right before she started Tetracycline. She has enough formula for the flight and until I get there.

ARIANA: Antibiotics won't slow it down. Your wife will make plenty of milk. Believe me, I know.

ABDULLAH: Thank you. But this breast milk is to give our baby until the antibiotics are out of her system.

ARIANA: How much longer will she be taking the medication?

ABDULLAH: Another week.

ARIANA: (*Giving contents of container a very cursory glance.*) That's nothing to worry about. The baby will be fine on formula for another week. And there's way more than three ounces in here.

ABDULLAH: I do not see a problem.

   (*Pulling sheets of paper from pocket.*)

I have printed this. To show you.

ARIANA: Is that a staple? You heard me say to empty *all metal* from your pockets.

ABDULLAH: I'm sorry. I forgot the staple. See? This is from your TSA. Transportation Security Administration.

   (*Reading from paper.*)

A new public law. Passed December 16, 2016, by President Obama. Called the BABES Act, the—

ARIANA: . . . Bottles and Breastfeeding Equipment Screening Act. I know. We got training on it.

ABDULLAH: Yes, so —?

ARIANA: So? You said you're traveling to London.

ABDULLAH: Yes, yes. I tell you that already.

ARIANA: UK regulations say parents can take breast milk on a plane if baby travels *with* the parent. Unless you've got one stashed in your luggage or that cooler, I don't see a baby traveling with you.

ABDULLAH: (*Removing additional sheets of paper.*) Please, if you would read this—

ARIANA: You're holding up the line. You need to step aside, so other passengers can get through. Let me x-ray this first.

(*Calling out.*)

Harry, could you take over for me here?

(*Carrying plastic bin and Styrofoam container, she points toward side of stage.*)

Wait over there. I'll be back in a minute.

(*He moves to side of stage. She exits briefly, then returns with bin and container.*)

ABDULLAH: (*Referring to second sheet of paperwork.*) If you please, this says here —

ARIANA: Another staple? What is it about no metal you don't understand?

ABDULLAH: I'm sorry. I forgot about the staples.

ARIANA: Let me see your passport.

ABDULLAH: (*Reaching into bin, grabs jacket, removes passport from pocket.*) Here it is.

ARIANA: Abdullah . . . Farooq?

ABDULLAH: That is my name.

ARIANA: Sit down, please. Are you an American citizen?

ABDULLAH: Of course. This is my American passport.

ARIANA: Does that mean you also have another passport from somewhere else?

ABDULLAH: No. Only this one.

ARIANA: Where were you born?

ABDULLAH: Here.

ARIANA: At JFK airport?

ABDULLAH: New Jersey. I was born in New Jersey. Newark.

ARIANA: What about your parents?

ABDULLAH: They were also born in New Jersey. Please, may I ask, what is the problem?

ARIANA: (*Muttering and looking at passport.*) Christ, it's like New Jersey is turning into a third world country.

    (*Pause.*)

Abdullah Farooq. That's a Muslim name, right?

ABDULLAH: Yes, I am Muslim.

    (*Peering at her name tag.*)

Ariana. Your name is Ariana. That is also a Muslim name. It means full of life. Vivacious.

ARIANA: It is not—

ABDULLAH: Your name is also the name of an airline. Ariana Airlines. The national airline of Afghanistan.

ARIANA: My parents did *not* name me for some airline in Afghanistan.

ABDULLAH: (*Reading from the second set of papers.*) I printed this, just in case. "New Regulations within UK: February 8, 2017. Passengers carrying breast milk may carry an unlimited supply. They do *not* have to be accompanied by the infant."

ARIANA: That's passengers traveling *within* the UK. Not *to* the UK.

ABDULLAH: (*Checking his watch.*) Oh . . .But —?

ARIANA: I've never seen a *man* trying to get breast milk through security before except—

ABDULLAH: I have explained to you—

ARIANA: . . . this one time. Someone self-identifying as a woman. With a baby. A guy saying *he* was the baby's mother. We had to let him. . . her . . . whatever . . . through. He had formula, thought, not breast milk. Are you a man who self-identifies as a woman? We had training to—

ABDULLAH: I am a normal American father. Don't treat me as though I were some Eskimo or—

ARIANA: You can't call them Eskimos any longer. You have to call them Inuits. We had training . . .

ABDULLAH: You're a mother . . .

ARIANA: I'm also a TSA agent responsible for keeping passengers safe. And for keeping the line moving so passengers don't miss their flights.

ABDULLAH: (*Pushing button on mobile phone.*) Here is our new baby. Our son.

ARIANA: How do I know that's really your wife and son?

ABDULLAH: But . . . look at his eyes . . . his chin . . . he looks just like me. How old are your children?

ARIANA: (*Softening, but only a little bit.*) Not that it's any of your business, but two and six. Do you have his birth certificate with you?

ABDULLAH: No one told me I needed it. Do you have pictures of your children?

ARIANA: Look, we're busy here . . .

ABDULLAH: You must miss them when you're at work all day. We're away from the others. They can't see.

ARIANA: (*Sighs, pulls out mobile phone and shows him picture of children.*) Here. My two reasons for living.

ABDULLAH: How beautiful they are!

ARIANA: (*Softening—a bit more.*) Yeah. They're good kids.

ABDULLAH: My wife, she had a difficult labor. Then her respiratory illness. Two other children, a new baby, her mother in the hospital. It is too much to for her to handle by herself.

ARIANA: Three kids and a sick mother? Jeez . . . I can't imagine . . . She's lucky to have you to help.

ABDULLAH: As a mother yourself, I'm sure you understand why they need me.

ARIANA: As a passenger, I'm sure you realize it's my duty to protect other passengers from—

ABDULLAH: Of course. These are dangerous times we live in. Please, what can I do to—?

ARIANA: (*opening Styrofoam cooler, looking in it.*) Okay, okay, let me see . . . hey, wait. This stuff is frozen.

ABDULLAH: Yes, I told you that. My wife put it there to keep fresh.

(*ARIANA reaches for frozen package of breast milk.*)

May I ask you to please wear gloves when handling —?

ARIANA: Oh, for Christ's sake!

(*She snaps on a pair of latex gloves.*)

ABDULLAH: Thank you. These papers also say it's against the law for you to make me taste it, but I will do so if it makes you more comfortable. Or, perhaps you could discuss this with your supervisor?

ARIANA: I *am* the supervisor.

ABDULLAH: Congratulations. Your husband and children must be very proud of you.

ARIANA: (*Sighing.*) What husband?

ABDULLAH: I am sorry. It should be a father's duty as well as his pleasure to support his wife and children.

ARIANA: (*Sighing again—a big one this time.*) Ha! That'll be the day.

(*Pause.*)

I'm sorry. We cannot allow you to bring this on the plane.

ABDULLAH: Why not? Can't you test it?

ARIANA: This milk is frozen, so any testing would be inconclusive. Your wife should have refrigerated it, then packed it with ice packs to keep it cool. Didn't you check our website?

ABDULLAH: We didn't know . . . but you x-rayed it. You saw that there's no metal in—

ARIANA: Wouldn't alter our decision.

(*Pause.*)

Look, don't worry. If your wife just had a baby, she'll still be lactating when she's finished with antibiotics. How old is the baby?

ABDULLAH: Only two months.

ARIANA: Then she'll have enough milk to supply a dairy farm. Believe me, I know.

ABDULLAH: Oh. I didn't know.

ARIANA: Three kids and you know nothing about lactating mothers?

ABDULLAH: That's between the mother and baby. Why would you think my wife's breast milk is suspicious?

ARIANA: (*Hesitating.*) Well . . . uh . . . it's because . . .I mean . . . you're . . . you're . . . you know . . . I mean . . .

ABDULLAH: Because I'm a man?

ARIANA: That's part of it. No baby.

ABDULLAH: But I showed you his picture . . .

ARIANA: It could be anybody's baby . . . and you're . . . you're . . . I mean . . . you know . . . a . . .

ABDULLAH: A man who happens to be a Muslim?

ARIANA: . . . well . . . to be honest . . . yes.

ABDULLAH: Your organization is discriminating against me, a second-generation American citizen? If I were a black woman or a white man or Buddhist monk, would there be a problem?

ARIANA: I really couldn't say. Each case is a separate—

ABDULLAH: This country advocates for tolerance and diversity. And you,

you work for the American government. Yet you profile me because of my gender and my religion? That is not fair.

ARIANA: You're free to discuss it with customer service. I'll give you the website. But right now, the line is getting longer, and you need to either leave the area or leave the milk and go through security.

ABDULLAH: What about my wife's milk? My baby—

ARIANA: You can't take it through security. Sorry.

(*Softening.*)

Listen, it'll be okay. The baby will do fine on formula until your wife stops her medication.

ABDULLAH: But the milk? What will you do with it?

ARIANA: Dispose of it once it thaws.

ABDULLAH: Dispose of it. Just like that. People in other countries are starving, and you just —

ARIANA: (*Moving away.*) Sir, you need to either leave the milk or leave the area. We're getting backed up.

ABDULLAH: (*Checks watch, puts jacket, shoes, and belt back on. Picks up Styrofoam container.*) If my friend hasn't left the parking lot, I'll give him this to refreeze. It is wrong to throw it out.

ARIANA: (*Softening again.*) I guess.

(*Pause.*)

I'm really sorry about this. Hope you don't miss your flight.

(*ARIANA turns away, moves to one side of stage. ABDULLAH carries Styrofoam container to opposite side of stage, removes mobile phone, punches in numbers.*)

ARIANA: (*To unseen colleague.*) God, Harry. I feel so guilty. He was such a nice guy. New baby. Worried about his wife. I don't have anything against them . . . Muslims, I mean. He's American. Born in New Jersey. But they just promoted me . . . I don't want to mess up . . . Do you think I did the right thing?

ABDULLAH: (*On phone. He no longer has any accent. Most likely, he's not even a Muslim.*) Hi. Homeland Security Red Team, JFK British Airways reporting back.

(*Pause.*)

Fine, fine. No, nothing got through. She even found the staples . . .

ARIANA: (*Offstage, to unseen colleague.*) . . .remember how I got chewed out when I almost let that old lady through with cuticle scissors?

ABDULLAH: (*On phone.*) . . . for someone who knows nothing about kids, I did a terrific imitation of a worried father . . . a bit of fidgeting, staring, y'know, in case she was doing that body language profiling bullshit . . .

ARIANA: (*To unseen colleague.*) . . . and I didn't mean to give that diabetic guy a hard time with his syringes, but then they said it was okay to let him through. Jesus, either way, you can't win . . .

ABDULLAH: (*On phone.*) . . . profiling is flawed science anyhow. She passed with flying colors. But you never know . . .

ARIANA: (*Offstage to unseen colleague.*) . . . then I thought, these are scary times we live in. But you never know . . .

(*Blackout.*)

MISS IRRELEVANT

by Jeff Stolzer

Workshop production
Sugartown Shorts
June 30, 2018
Bushwick, Brooklyn

Director, Jeff Stolzer
Actors, Bryn Packard and Nilsa Reyna

Full production
Untold Stories
Pleasance Theatre
November 10-11, 2018
London, England

Artistic directors, Mark Lindow and Emma Zadow
Director, Alan Phillips.

CHARLIE WEEMS, Kingsley Amadi
AMY STERLING, Emma Zadow

CHARACTERS

CHARLIE WEEMS, 40, M, a handsome, charismatic, recently-retired
 football star
AMY STERLING, 37, F, an attractive, former schoolmate of Charlie's.

SETTING

The book-signing area of a large bookstore.

TIME

Present day.

*LIGHTS UP. A large table center stage, on top of which sits a plastic sleeve with
the cover of a book,* Charlie Hero. *It features a photo of a handsome middle-
aged man, along with an archival photo of a quarterback signaling a touch-
down. Behind the table sits that man, CHARLIE WEEMS, 40, fit, megawatt
smile, well dressed. A woman approaches the table—this is AMY STERLING,
37, attractive but a little nervous.*

CHARLIE: Looks like you're Miss Irrelevant.

AMY: (*Confused.*) Excuse me?

CHARLIE: The last one in line.

AMY: I don't understand—

CHARLIE: (*All smooth charm.*) The last player taken in the NFL Draft every
year is called Mister Irrelevant, so I was just making a joke.

AMY: Oh.

CHARLIE: I didn't mean to insult you—I'm nothing if not a gentleman.

   (*She produces a copy of the book.*)

AMY: Great title.

CHARLIE: That was my nickname in college.

AMY: I remember.

   (*He gestures for her to hand the book to him and she does.*)

CHARLIE: How do you want it inscribed?

AMY: I read in the paper they want you to run for Senate.

CHARLIE: (*Smiling.*) We've had some discussions. I think the lessons you learn on the gridiron also apply to serving in Congress.

AMY: And those would be?

CHARLIE: Preparation, leadership, humility.

AMY: Ah, yes.

CHARLIE: And between you and me, I'm ready for that to be my next challenge in life. I hope to have your support.

AMY: (*Smiling.*) We'll see.

CHARLIE: Fair enough. So how do you want it inscribed?

AMY: To me.

CHARLIE: And your name would be?

AMY: You don't remember it?

CHARLIE: Remember it?

AMY: We were at State together.

CHARLIE: Let me think . . . .

AMY: Amy Sterling.

CHARLIE: (*Lying.*) Oh yes, Amy. It's nice to see you again.

AMY: Is it really?

CHARLIE: Sure.

AMY: You don't remember me, do you?

CHARLIE: Okay, you got me. There were 30,000 students at State and that was twenty years ago, so-

AMY: You were a senior and I was freshman. You approached me in the cafeteria.

CHARLIE: I did?

AMY: Yes. We talked and you asked me out.

CHARLIE: Okay . . . .

AMY: Is it coming back now?

CHARLIE: (*Lying.*) Yes, a little.

AMY: I heard afterwards they had a nickname for me in your fraternity house.

CHARLIE: A nickname?

AMY: I heard they had nicknames for all the girls who came by the house and mine was . . . The Bod.

(*A flash of recognition on his face.*)

AMY: Now you remember me, don't you?

(*CHARLIE smiles and shrugs.*)

AMY: We dated for about a month.

CHARLIE: Right.

AMY: And then we stopped dating.

CHARLIE: Well, we were young-

AMY: Actually, you broke up with me.

CHARLIE: You know how those things go.

AMY: You called me the day after we had sex for the first time and you broke up with me.

CHARLIE: I don't remember-

AMY: Actually, it was the first time we had sex together and the first time I ever had sex.

CHARLIE: I'm sorry—

AMY: You weren't sorry then.

CHARLIE: I wasn't?

AMY: No. Don't you remember what happened that night?

CHARLIE: I . . . I don't.

AMY: You took me to a party in your frat house and you kept pouring shots of Jager for me.

CHARLIE: Those parties were pretty wild.

AMY: And I really wasn't used to drinking, I grew up in a dry county. But you kept pouring the shots and you got your frat brothers to cheer me on.

CHARLIE: (*Starting to squirm.*) Well—

AMY: They kept chanting "Amy, Amy" and you put the shots up to my lips and I really didn't have much of a choice.

CHARLIE: Oh, come on—that was all part of the fun back then.

AMY: It wasn't fun when I got sick and threw up.

CHARLIE: I'm sorry.

AMY: So you said that was enough and took me up to your room.

CHARLIE: Yes, I realized . . . I realized things had gone too far and I'm always a gentleman so I took you up to my room to get away from there.

AMY: So the "gentleman" took me up to his room and started kissing me and pushed me down on the bed and forced himself on me.

CHARLIE: That's . . . that's not how I remember it.

AMY: Oh, you remember that but you didn't even remember my name.

CHARLIE: I . . . I remember we had a good time.

AMY: Rapists always think it's a good time.

CHARLIE: Please don't call me that.

AMY: And maybe it is a good time—for them.

CHARLIE: No.

AMY: For you.

CHARLIE: No.

AMY: For you, the rapist.

CHARLIE: Don't call me that.

AMY: If the shoe fits—

CHARLIE: No.

AMY: Or maybe I should say . . . the cleat.

CHARLIE: Stop.

AMY: It's what you are.

CHARLIE: No.

AMY: If you rape a woman, that makes you a rapist.

CHARLIE: This is ridiculous.

AMY: I told you I was a virgin and didn't want to have sex with you but you pinned me down on the bed and you raped me anyway.

CHARLIE: I . . . I . . . We just have different memories of what happened!

AMY: You raped me and then you broke up with me.

CHARLIE: Why would I do that?

AMY: To impress your frat brothers. Sandy told me it was quite the big story in the house that you had "banged The Bod."

CHARLIE: Who's Sandy?

AMY: Sandy London. She was my roommate.

CHARLIE: How did she—

AMY: She dated Dave Ferguson at the end of freshman year. You remember Dave.

CHARLIE: Well, sure—he was the president of the house.

AMY: Dave told Sandy that you were proud as a peacock to have "The Bod" as a notch on your belt.

CHARLIE: Look, I was a kid back then—

AMY: You were twenty-one. You were an adult. I was seventeen. I was the kid.

CHARLIE: What do you want me to say—I'm sorry?

AMY: Are you sorry?

CHARLIE: Of course I'm sorry.

AMY: What are you sorry for?

CHARLIE: I'm sorry . . . I'm sorry that whatever happened back then upset you.

AMY: "Whatever happened?"

CHARLIE: Yes.

AMY: You raped me.

CHARLIE: That's not what happened.

AMY: Then I don't accept your non-apology. And as for "upsetting me" . . . well that is the understatement of the century.

CHARLIE: Meaning . . . ?

AMY: (*Very emotional.*) Meaning I blamed myself and developed an eating disorder and I was down to seventy pounds and almost died. I had to take a leave of absence and it took me two full years to recover!

CHARLIE: And that's all because of me?

AMY: Because of you and what you did.

CHARLIE: Nothing like taking personal responsibility.

AMY: Says the rapist who can't apologize for raping.

(*CHARLIE tries to hand back the book.*)

CHARLIE: We'll just have to agree to disagree.

(*She refuses to take it.*)

AMY: Or we can just let the voters decide.

CHARLIE: (*Alarmed.*) What?

AMY: Let them decide if your preparation, leadership, humility, and raping qualify you to be a Senator.

CHARLIE: So that's what this is about.

AMY: It sure is.

CHARLIE: How much?

AMY: How much?

CHARLIE: How much money do you want to stay silent?

AMY: I just want the voters to know the truth.

CHARLIE: I'll deny it. It will be he said, she said.

AMY: Maybe. But I have a book of my own.

(She pulls out an old, tattered diary from her pocketbook.)

I wrote everything down in this diary when it happened. And I told Sandy—
she'll verify my story.

*(CHARLIE stands up, filled with anger—he wants to grab her. He looks
around and realizes there isn't anything he can do in this public setting.)*

And we know about the other girls you raped when you were in the NFL—
the ones you paid off in return for confidentiality agreements.

CHARLIE: How . . . how do you know about them?!

AMY: Actually we didn't. I was bluffing. But you just confirmed it, Senator.

CHARLIE: You crazy bitch—I'll just deny it.

AMY: We don't think that will be credible.

CHARLIE: Who is this "we"?

(AMY gestures behind her.)

AMY: Sandy London and me. That's Sandy way back in the corner over
there. Wave to him, Sandy.

(Charlie's reaction indicates she waved.)

CHARLIE: What-the-fuck?

AMY: Sandy is a producer for CNN.

(Gesturing to her blazer.)

This button is actually a small camera and this one has a tiny microphone. Everything has been recorded.

(CHARLIE is shocked. AMY starts to walk away, then turns back.)

By the way, in November . . . I wouldn't count on the support of Miss Irrelevant.

(She exits. CHARLIE glowers, then hangs his head.)

(Lights out.)

MOTHS

by Don Nigro

CHARACTERS

MEREDITH CHERRY, a woman of 34
BEN PALESTRINA, a man of 20

TIME

Summer of 1970.

SETTING

A back porch on a summer night in Armitage, a small town in the hilly part of East Ohio. BEN and MEREDITH sitting on a porch swing. Sound of crickets. Fireflies.

MEREDITH: You came to see me.

BEN: Of course I did.

MEREDITH: I thought you'd forget me.

BEN: Nobody can forget you.

MEREDITH: Many have tried.

BEN: Not me. How are you?

MEREDITH: I sit out here every night, watching the moths flying against the porch screen, trying to get to the light. The screen stops them. They don't understand. But they keep trying. They're like people. Stupid, but persistent. (*Pause.*) You look good. More grown-up.

BEN: You look beautiful.

MEREDITH: I'm fourteen years older than you.

BEN: You haven't changed at all.

MEREDITH: I'm always changing. (*Pause.*) I know a secret.

BEN: What's that?

MEREDITH: You've got to promise not to tell my father.

BEN: All right.

MEREDITH: It's about the moths.

BEN: What about them?

MEREDITH: Each one of the moths that comes to the back porch at night when I'm sitting on the porch swing, watching the fireflies, each one of those moths is actually the soul of something.

BEN: The soul of what?

MEREDITH: They're ghosts. Moths are ghosts. And at night they come for you.

BEN: They're attracted to the light.

MEREDITH: But they come for you. They want to get in the house so that when you're asleep they can crawl in your ears and get into your dreams.

BEN: How do you know this?

MEREDITH: Because I listen.

BEN: You listen to what?

MEREDITH: I listen to the crickets. The crickets are trying to warn me. To watch out for the moths. And the fireflies are warning me, the way they flicker on and off in the dark, the patterns they make in the dark. Because once the moths get into your head, they start nibbling away at your brain, from inside your skull. And as they nibble away more and more of your brain, they uncover buried memories, like digging up pieces of broken crockery or old bones in the back garden, out behind the shed, in that patch of ferns. The moths that get into your brain, the ghost moths that haunt the inside of your head are engaged in a sort of archaeology of memories. And these are memories you don't want dug up. Bad memories you spend years trying to bury in your head, but also good ones, that hurt even worse because they're memories of things you can't ever get back. The ghost moths get into your brain and eat away the insulation and uncover the memories and you start to go mad again.

BEN: I don't think that's going to happen.

MEREDITH: Of course you don't. There's nobody more ignorant than sane people. (*Pause.*) My daughter's in love with you.

BEN: No she's not.

MEREDITH: Yes she is. I can tell. She adores you.

BEN: Your daughter is fifteen. I'm too old for her.

MEREDITH: You're only twenty.

BEN: When she's fifteen, that's too old.

MEREDITH: Not in her mind.

BEN: She's a wonderful girl. Very smart. Boys will be following her around everywhere. You're going to have to beat them off with a stick.

MEREDITH: That's what I'm afraid of. They followed me around like that, and look what happened. Boys are not entirely human.

BEN: She'll be okay. She can take care of herself. She's smarter than they are.

MEREDITH: Nobody can take care of themselves. Nobody can take care of anybody. (*Pause.*) Maybe you'll marry her, when she's older.

BEN: I don't think so.

MEREDITH: Do you still have that girlfriend, at college?

BEN: Yes.

MEREDITH: Is she insane?

BEN: I don't think so. Maybe a little.

MEREDITH: It's my fault, you know.

BEN: What is?

MEREDITH: I'm the first girl you ever made love to. I put a little bit of the dark world in your head. Now you're always going to love girls who are just a little bit insane.

BEN: Everybody is a little bit insane.

MEREDITH: Ben, I'm terrified for her.

BEN: Why?

MEREDITH: I'm terrified she'll be like me.

BEN: She is like you. She's smart and beautiful and funny and strong and very independent and absolutely unique.

MEREDITH: Yes. Many of the craziest people in the world are like that. My mother was like that. She ran off, and my father's been broken ever since. Nothing can fix him.

BEN: Your father loves you very much.

MEREDITH: That's the problem. Love is always the problem. I'm just like my mother, and now I'm scared my daughter will be just like me. And she'll seem perfectly fine. And then one day, maybe when she's about your age, the moths will get into her head, and they'll start eating her brain.

BEN: That's not going to happen.

MEREDITH: Don't tell me it's not going to happen. You don't know it's not going to happen.

BEN: I don't think it's going to happen.

MEREDITH: But you don't know. (*Pause.*) I've been out for six months.

BEN: Your father says you're doing fine.

MEREDITH: It always seems like I'm doing fine, at first. I'm very good at seeming fine. My brain is calmer than it was. They keep switching the medication. They don't know what the hell they're doing, but every once in a while something works. For a time. But late at night, lying in bed alone, here in my father's house. I can feel the moths. Nibbling at the inside of my head. Unearthing memories. The moths do this on purpose, to drive you insane with grief.

BEN: Why would they do that?

MEREDITH: Because they are the souls of all the creatures who've died so you could live. They are the revenants of everything you've ever eaten, and everybody whose place you took on earth. There's only so much room on earth. So everybody who's alive now has taken the place of somebody else who died. Or there wouldn't be enough food. That's how it works. And the job of the moths is to uncover all these memories, and fill you with so much grief that you want to die.

BEN: You don't want to die.

MEREDITH: I've tried. The first time, you tried to save me, and you almost drowned yourself. Foolish boy. Jumping in the water to try and save me when you couldn't swim. Don't you know that nobody can save anybody? You're going to spend your whole life trying to save people who can't be saved and don't want to be saved, and they'll punish you for it, like I did.

BEN: You never did that. You lived, and you had a beautiful daughter, who loves you very much.

MEREDITH: Promise me something.

BEN: What?

MEREDITH: Promise me you'll never sleep with my daughter.

BEN: Meredith.

MEREDITH: I'm serious. I mean it. Promise me. You've got to promise me. No matter how beautiful she gets when she's all grown up, you've got to promise me you'll never, ever sleep with her. No matter how much she begs you. Because she's already in love with you. I can tell.

BEN: I promise you I will never sleep with your daughter.

MEREDITH: But always watch out for her.

BEN: I'll watch out for her.

MEREDITH: You can't save her, but you can watch out for her, and maybe put off for a while the day when the moths start eating her brain.

BEN: She'll have you to look out for her, too.

MEREDITH: I don't know if I can. Because the moths have told me that soon I'm going to end up back in that place. And this time maybe I'll never come out again. I need you to do this for me. Take care of my daughter and never, never sleep with her. No matter how much you want to. Because you will want to. Because she'll remind you of me.

BEN: Meredith, she's going to be fine, and so are you.

MEREDITH: Swear it to me. Swear to me that you'll always look out for her and never sleep with her. Because love is the foundation of all sorrow. The moths told me. They whisper it to me over and over in the night. So you've got to swear. Do you swear?

BEN: I swear.

MEREDITH: Do you love this girl of yours, at college?

BEN: Yes.

MEREDITH: Does she love you?

BEN: Yes. I think so.

MEREDITH: That's very sad.

BEN: Sometimes it is.

MEREDITH: Nothing ever ends well.

BEN: I suppose.

MEREDITH: The moths have told me. Love is what kills you. And the moths come, every night, to remind you that you owe somebody else a death. (*Pause.*) It might be better for her if I was dead.

BEN: It would not be better for her if you were dead.

MEREDITH: You really don't think so?

BEN: She needs you.

MEREDITH: But she can't trust me not to be crazy.

BEN: She can trust you to love her. That she can trust. And she needs that. So stop thinking about dying.

MEREDITH: I'll try. (*Pause.*) Also, I worry that when I'm dead I won't be able to stay away. I'll come back as one of the moths. And I'll get into her head. And I'll start digging up memories, like broken fragments of old crockery. (*Pause.*) Do you still love me?

BEN: Very much.

MEREDITH: No matter what?

BEN: No matter what.

MEREDITH: Be careful who you love.

BEN: Who you love is not something a person chooses.

MEREDITH: Just don't let me in, okay? When I come to your back porch at night, flapping against the screen, don't let me in. Don't ever let me in.

(*BEN reaches out and holds her hand. They hold hands and watch the fireflies. The light fades on them and goes out.*)

NEVERTHELESS SHE PERSISTED

by Richard Dresser

First production by
Dreamcatcher Repertory Theatre
120 Morris Avenue
Summit, New Jersey 07901
April 26–May 13, 2018

Director, Laura Ekstrand

CAREY, Amanda Salazar
MORGAN, Ben Kaufman
JEN, Beth Painter
BOB, Michael Aquino

CHARACTERS

CAREY, a woman 30–45, more appalled with every passing day at what is happening in the world outside her home.

MORGAN, her husband, possibly older, trying to keep things on an even keel.

JEN, 30–45, an old friend of CAREY'S, struggling with a diminished household budget.

BOB, JEN's husband, newly unemployed, looking for a scapegoat.

SETTING

The living room of CAREY and MORGAN's comfortable suburban home.

TIME

Friday night, a little later than they thought.

CAREY and MORGAN and BOB and JEN enter the living room after several magical hours in the dining room. They're glowing with alcohol and good cheer.

JEN: I had no idea it was so late!

CARÉY: Don't even joke about leaving—

BOB: We actually do have to go. This has been—

MORGAN: It always is with you guys. Always—

CAREY: And we didn't talk about *him*.

BOB: Thank god . . .

JEN: Everything was amazing. The salmon and the kale salad and the dessert—

BOB: That fucking cobbler!

CAREY: Will you do us a favor and take that fucking cobbler?

JEN: No! We'd just eat it and hate ourselves.

CAREY: Well we can't have it in the house. It's like crack. I have absolutely no willpower and Morgan has less. I'm going to pack it up for you.

MORGAN: Before you do . . .

CAREY: What?

MORGAN: I feel the need to say something.

BOB: Fight it, Morgan, fight that need.

JEN: Morgan's going to give a little speech and we should just accept that.

BOB: Would you look at the time? We really *do* have to go—

MORGAN: Calm down. This will be short. But as you reflect on it over the coming years it will make you joyful.

CAREY: It's so much better if someone else says that, dear.

JEN: Bring it, dude.

MORGAN: At times like this . . . actually there have never been times like this, when six months of news gets crammed into every day and our brains are literally changing to accommodate the avalanche of horror and deceit—

CAREY: We're not talking about him, remember?

JEN: But Morgan's right, we're not who we were. I'm certainly not—

BOB: Wait your turn, babe, this is Morgan's little speech.

JEN: I'm just saying we're all suffering from PTSD.

MORGAN: Except that would suggest the trauma is over. And it isn't. The silver lining of this Age of Abomination is that we know what truly matters and we treasure it more than ever. For me, the only way I'll survive is with good friends. I can't imagine living in a world without Bob and Jen.

JEN: Thank you, Morgan. We feel the same way.

CAREY: So where do I fit in?

BOB: Uh-oh . . . you fucked up your little speech, Morgan. Forgot about your bride . . .

MORGAN: I'd be nothing without you, sweetheart. You know that.

CAREY: I do know that.

MORGAN: Good. Because it's true. How would you be without me?

CAREY: You know, I think I'd be okay. I'd be sad but after a few weeks I'd discover that I'm stronger than I thought. And a brand new life would open up for me.

MORGAN: Yikes. I'll be sure to give you a shout-out in my next little speech.

CAREY: Whatever. I'll grab that cobbler. No way do you two leave without it.

    (CAREY goes to the dining room.)

BOB: I'm going to warm up the car. Just for you, sweetheart.

JEN: You are such a doll! Isn't it great it's so cold, the way it used to be?

(*MORGAN tosses BOB his coat. BOB exits outside. CAREY enters with the cobbler.*)

JEN: Oh, boy. We'll probably just gobble it down in the car like animals. Can you possibly give me the recipe?

CAREY: Sure, it's my mom's. She's been turning up in my dreams, like, every night. It's crazy.

JEN: I could tell Bob really wanted the cobbler but he wouldn't admit it. I mean we're all going to die so what's wrong with feeling good sometimes? I caught him running on the treadmill eating a jelly donut.

CAREY: He looks good, he really does—

JEN: Just eat the fucking donut, Bob!

CAREY: But he's okay, right? I mean he's . . . good?

JEN: He needed this, he needed tonight. No tension for a change.

MORGAN: There's never any tension when we get together. Is there?

JEN: No! But . . . he just can't relax anymore.

CAREY: Even around us? *Us?* I mean look at us!

MORGAN: We invented relaxing . . . we have the patent . . .

JEN: It's not you. But sometimes things get said that get heard in a way that wasn't maybe the way they were actually intended to be said.

MORGAN: Whoa, I can't remember . . . did we smoke some weed?

JEN: I'm sorry, I'm not very articulate.

CAREY: Was it a mistake talking about school? Shit! You don't even *want* your kids in private school anymore . . . and you know what? I totally agree!

JEN: Can we just drop it?

CAREY: Drop what?

JEN: I never should have brought up the tension thing. He's in a bit of a rough patch. No job—

MORGAN: I thought he was consulting—

JEN: Oh, please, that's just a euphemism for racquetball and PornHub. If I weren't working . . .

CAREY: Honestly, it doesn't surprise me. The tension. It's actually kind of obvious.

JEN: What are you talking about?

CAREY: Well . . . you know that thing Bob does?

(BOB has entered.)

BOB: What does Bob do?

CAREY: (*Off the group stare.*) Fuck. I'm sorry. It's nothing. Do we have to do this?

MORGAN: Apparently we do.

CAREY: Okay . . . sitting next to you, Bob . . . when I look away for a second or give a slight indication that you don't have my absolute full attention?

BOB: What do I do?

CAREY: You hit me.

BOB: Excuse me?

CARRIE: Not hard. Like this.

(Demonstrates how BOB taps her arm.)

Like you're afraid I'm not listening.

BOB: I was hitting you?

CAREY: Not *hitting* hitting. Tapping . . .
BOB: This is pretty weird, Carey. Even for you. Do I do that, babe?

JEN: Don't drag me into this.

BOB: I'd like to know if I hit people. Maybe it's hurting me professionally. Like maybe that's why I can't get a fucking job. Someone's interviewing me and *whack*! I hit 'em.

JEN: I wasn't aware you did that, Bob.

BOB: Morgan?

MORGAN: I didn't see anything . . .

CAREY: Coward.

BOB: Carey, if you think I hit you I'm sorry.

CAREY: "If you're upset I grabbed your ass in the elevator then I apologize." You should run for office . . .

MORGAN: Stop it! Jesus! Why are you attacking Bob?

CAREY: I'm not attacking Bob. It's just . . . we all have strange things we do. I know I do . . .

BOB: And I do too. But I don't do that.

JEN: And if you do it's an unconscious thing.

CAREY: See, Bob? Jen knows. And Morgan knows even though he won't cop to it.

JEN: Why does it matter, Carey? Really.

CAREY: It matters because the truth matters. The truth is under assault and every time we accept a lie, even a small stupid one, we are destroying this fragile life we love so much. So can we just tell the fucking truth? Is that too much to ask?

BOB: I am telling the truth. I don't hit people who don't listen.

CAREY See, this is the problem. This is what *he* does. The truth is whatever he wants it to be.

JEN: Do not do that. Do not compare Bob to *him*.

CAREY: He invades every corner of our lives with his aggressive ignorance and just blurts out whatever the hell he feels like saying and sixty million people believe this pathological liar—

MORGAN: I thought we weren't going to talk about him . . .

CAREY: And women, God help me, they see who he is and what he does and they still love him . . .

BOB: Do you want me to explain why they still love him?

CAREY: Yes, Bob, would you please man-splain women to me?

BOB: He speaks the truth.

JEN: Ohmygod, Bob . . .

CAREY: He lies the way actual humans breathe . . .

BOB: But with all the lies . . . there's a deeper truth, a primitive truth. He's a vulgar, frightened, weak, loveless, bully trapped in an absurd cartoon carcass with hair of a color not found in nature. He's lost and angry and spiteful and dishonest. He's us.

CAREY: He's not us! He's not you and he's not me—

BOB: All of us with our endless needs. Which we try to hide with decency and compassion and logic but our needs are always there. The pathetic, bottomless needs of an abandoned child. But he doesn't hide *his* needs. He puts 'em out there for all to see. And it's staggering and perverse and we can't look away because it's the worst, sickest part of us, he's everything we fight so hard to hide. And he doesn't give a fuck. The way we wish we could face the day, just not giving a fuck. He is us and we are him.

CAREY: I love you, Bob, but you're wrong.

BOB: Have you ever noticed how often the word "love" is followed by the word "but?"

CAREY: We're better than that.

BOB: We sure do like to think so. You say you want the truth, Carey. But you're working your ass off not to see it when it's right in front of you, staring you down.

CAREY: So where does that leave us? With no hope? Nothing . . . ?

MORGAN: We have our friends.

JEN: Who really do need to go. The sitter's making a fortune tonight . . .

CAREY: Oh, dear. You'll take the cobbler?

JEN: Thanks, Carey. I wish I'd met your mom.

CAREY: I keep dreaming about her. Holding my hand crossing the street. Telling me I'm too sick to go to school. Keeping me warm and cozy and . . . safe. We're good, right?

JEN: Of course, sweetie!

BOB: The driveway's pretty slick. Have you got any salt to put down?

MORGAN: Damn! I meant to pick some up . . . but it's been warm for so long I forgot . . .

BOB: No sweat. We'll take our chances.

CAREY: Look, I'm sorry, Bob, I didn't mean . . .

BOB: No, I know.

CAREY: I wake up with Morning Joe and read the TIMES and the POST and all day long I check Politico and the Daily Beast and at night I watch Rachel while I'm on Facebook with everyone posting their daily outrage . . .

MORGAN: And she wonders why she can't sleep.

JEN: This *was so much fun*! Thanks for *everything*! What a lovely night!

   (BOB and JEN leave.)

CAREY: I'm such a fucking idiot.

MORGAN: No, honey, you're the best. I'm going to clean up. You chill out, finish your wine, it'll only take a minute . . .

   (He goes into the dining room. CAREY drinks her wine. She starts to cry.)

MORGAN: (*Offstage.*) I'm sorry I didn't mention you in my little speech.

CAREY: (*Brightly, above her tears.*) It's okay, I was just giving you a hard time!

MORGAN: (*Offstage.*) I know. I love you

CAREY: You too.

   (Softly.)

I can't do this anymore . . .

   (She is alone with her wine, lost.)

PAY IT BACKWARD

by Donna Hoke

First produced
Lakeshore Ten-Minute Play Festival
May 2018
Artistic Director, Ben Ratkowski

White Bear, MN

CHARACTERS

SAM, An office worker, on the younger side.
CHRIS, An officer worker, on the younger side.
TRACY, A visitor to the office, on the older side.

All roles can be played by the best actors you have available, regardless of gender or ethnicity.

SETTING

The present; the homespun offices of Random Acts of Kindness Credit Bureau, essentially a couple desks and some phones. This is not an office that gets visitors.

A sign reads: "Perform a RAK, We'll Pat Your Back." CHRIS at desk. SAM on phone. Phone rings constantly, and we go back and forth between CHRIS and SAM, as they rapidly field the calls, picking up as the other is talking, picking up with them mid-conversation, etc. Will take a little phone choreography but should move quickly with no lag time.

SAM: Random Acts of Kindness Credit Bureau. Paying tolls is always kind. Clichéd, but kind . . . Yes, *very* kind. Good job.

(Hangs up, immediately picks up.)

CHRIS: —One drop of soda isn't that much— Oh, your *last* drop. 100 degrees or not, that's kind of a backwash situation-

SAM: —Leaving money on a vending machine doesn't assure someone will buy a snack— They could take it and buy any number— Of course drugs—

CHRIS: —I don't know what to say, because, well . . . do you really think that quenched his thirst

(Hangs up, immediately picks up.)

SAM: —I see your point. Good drugs would make it a very kind act. You're a nice person.

(Hangs up, immediately picks up.)

CHRIS: —You don't have to come in. It's not a literal pat on the— Right. Attaboy! Good job!

(Hangs up, immediately picks up.)

SAM: —But you videotaped yourself saving the kitten— Well, then you shouldn't be calling here—

CHRIS: —I see. Oh no, I get that you just wanted to hold their baby so they could eat in peace, but that could seem like— Yes. A stalker—

SAM: —Right, this is for anonymous— No, random isn't anonymous . . . They're not mutually ex— . . . It can be anonymous and random or random and *not* anonymous—

(Reacts to rude hang up, picks up.)

CHRIS: —or a kidnapper, sure . . . . Paying for their lunch— Yes. Good save. Would you like to enroll in our Pay It Forward program?—

(He hangs up, immediately picks up.)

SAM: —But a thank you note by its very nature means—

CHRIS: —If someone *else* Instagrammed it . . . like the barefoot man who *got* your shoes . . . No, he probably doesn't have Instagram, but that doesn't change—

SAM: —It's on Facebook? Then it's not anonymous. Even with only seven— . . . I can't give you credit—

CHRIS: If the sign offering free dry cleaning is in your window . . . I don't know, it seems like you want people to *reward* you for being kind to unemployed— The thought never crossed your mind?

(He hangs up, picks up.)

SAM: Of course a like isn't as a good as a retweet, but it still doesn't—

CHRIS: But maybe the person who found the book won't think it was interesting— You can't assume— It doesn't matter who— Listen, I think you just wanted to unload the book!

(He reacts to a rude hang-up, picks up.)

SAM: —I just can't. I'm sorry you're not better liked.

(Hangs up, picks up.)

Random Acts of Kindness Credit Bureau.

CHRIS: Holding a door open is just—The person said thank you?—

SAM: —Let me ask my colleague . . .

(Covers the phone and says to CHRIS.)

This guy is dressing up as Batman and handing out sandwiches to the homeless, and he's been the news, but nobody knows it's him . . . does he get credit?

CHRIS: (*covering phone.*) I think the news piece counts as credit.

SAM: My colleague says you've already received credit—

(He hangs up.)

CHRIS: No, it doesn't count as a Pay It Forward!

(He hangs up. Break time; they both turn off their phones/switchboards/ whatever. CHRIS and SAM let out sighs.)

CHRIS: It's getting worse.

SAM: I long for the simple days of people leaving a penny at the register.

CHRIS: We need to drop the anonymous thing, let 'em double-dip on social media.

SAM: I like to imagine that there are people out there being   kind and *not* calling. Or posting.

CHRIS: That's a nice dream, Sam, but reality is these phones.

SAM: But our company is built on the idea of giving credit where it's due. Without anyone knowing.

CHRIS: Hey, I'm the one who came up with the illusion of selflessness, remember? But credit's too easy to come by now.

SAM: I say it in a human voice. I infuse my praise with love and sincere gratitude. Why is that not enough.

CHRIS: Because social media means no vetting! You can troll for credit for feeling bad about yourself, or losing an ounce, or "life being hard." Pats on the back without a single good deed. Quantity over quality. That's what we're up against.

SAM: But spreading kindness would make them feel better.

CHRIS: It's a tough sale.

SAM: If we don't drop the anonymous, we'll be out of business?

CHRIS: Dude, it's the whole kindness thing that's going down the tubes. We're just a casualty. Like Blockbuster.

(TRACY enters.)

TRACY: Is this the RAK Credit Bureau?

SAM: "Perform a RAK, we'll pat your back."

TRACY: You're Sam!

(She extends hand to shake SAM's.)

And you must be Chris! This is *so* exciting!

(*She vigorously pumps CHRIS's hand.*)

CHRIS: Can we help you with something?

TRACY: It's so nice to meet you in person! I usually only call.

SAM: You're a regular?

TRACY: You don't recognize my voice?

SAM: We get so many calls—

TRACY: Because it's such a wonderful thing you're doing. It makes it so much easier to decide, "Should I remind my neighbor it's garbage day?" It's nothing to me, but the thought of your "Good job!" spurs me on.

SAM: See, that's just what I—

TRACY: Or do I tell that man he's about to step in a big pile of dog poop? If I don't, it might be funny, you know? But then I hear your voice telling me, "You probably made that person's day," and it's worth it.

SAM: That's what we're here for, um—

TRACY: Tracy. And really, when I think about y'all, there's no question that I had to tip off the police about those little thugs mugging everyone on Turner Street.

CHRIS: That was you?

TRACY: It was! Don't you remember me calling yesterday?

SAM: I took that call. That was incredible. I mean, I think I got on a soapbox about your nobility, your innate sense of kindness, of justice, your—

TRACY: "You're a credit to humanity." Credit for being a credit, I saw what you did there.

CHRIS: How did you know who it was?

TRACY: People talk, I listen.

SAM: "So shines a good deed in a weary world."

TRACY: Huh?

SAM: Just knowing you saved people. Maybe lives. You must have felt so good about—

TRACY: Whatever. I *do* know I was on the phone with you for almost four minutes!

SAM: I can get a little overenthus—

TRACY: That's when I knew it was a really good one, and I probably had enough—

SAM: It was! See, Chris, maybe we're not obsolete. If we can inspire that kind of—

TRACY: —and that's why I'm here to collect.

CHRIS: Collect?

TRACY: My credit.

CHRIS: You got your credit. Every time you called. "Good job." "You made their day." "A credit to humanity." You said yourself—

TRACY: No, my actual credit.

SAM: I don't understand.

TRACY: I performed all these good deeds, and got credit. I'm ready to cash in. I need a good deed.

CHRIS: Um . . .

TRACY: Come on, my police tip-off was worth a lot.

CHRIS: It doesn't quite work that way.

TRACY: What do you mean?

CHRIS: The credit we give isn't that kind of credit.

TRACY: I don't follow.

CHRIS: It's verbal affirmation, not a deposit account.

TRACY: You mean there's no tit for tat?

CHRIS: I'm afraid not.

TRACY: Well, what the hell good is that?

SAM: It's external validation. That you're a good person. People seem to need that.

TRACY: Well, right now, I need someone to help me get rid of my husband.

CHRIS: Okay, whoa— Because that's not even—

TRACY: No, no, he's already gone.

SAM: Oh, no, you didn't—!

TRACY: No, no, he up and split, the damned hoarder! Took all the money and left all his crap! The whistles and backscratchers and presidential sugar packets and snot collection and—

CHRIS: The what?

TRACY: —troll dolls and Spider-Man costumes. It's too much for me to clear out. I have a bad back.

SAM: Perhaps some friends—

TRACY: Nope.

SAM: But surely someone—

TRACY: I posted it on Facebook.

SAM: But if they're your friends.

TRACY: Crickets.

SAM: They still should—

TRACY: This is why I was calling you! I was banking up the karma, so when I needed help I could get it. Turns out you're a coupla frauds.

CHRIS: Perhaps if you'd been enrolled in our Pay It Forward program—

TRACY: You're trying to upsell me now? Frauds!

CHRIS: Listen, nobody's trying to upsell you, because it's too late to enroll in Pay It Forward.

TRACY: What is it?

CHRIS: Oh now you want to—

SAM: It's simple, really. We just ask for a pledge from our callers that if somebody performs a RAK for them, they perform one in turn.

TRACY: Do they still get credit?\

SAM: Sure, but the point is—

TRACY: Real credit or your phony external validation credit?

CHRIS: If you're not interested in our programs—

TRACY: Your programs suck! You sit here all high and mighty deciding who's a nice person and who's not, and when a real person needs help, you can't be bothered. Then it's all "What have you done for us? You didn't enroll in our programs."

CHRIS: Listen, we provide a valuable service, and you can't just come in here—

TRACY: I'm sitting in your office with a genuine need for kindness, and you decide what? That I'm not *worthy*?

CHRIS: You're sitting there telling us the only reason you do anything nice is—

TRACY: At least I'm doing it! Which is more than I can say for you!

CHRIS: Me?! See Sam, this is exactly what I was trying to—

SAM: I'll do it. I'll help clean out the husband's stuff.

CHRIS: Why?!

TRACY: You will!?

(She digs in bag.)

SAM: I will.

CHRIS: Sam, you don't have to—

SAM: It's okay, Chris. I want to.

TRACY: See! I banked some karma after all. You are a good person.

(She extracts a card.)

Saturday would be great.

CHRIS: So maybe now I can interest you in Pay It Forward?

(TRACY hands SAM the card.)

TRACY: I'll think about it. See you Saturday!

(She exits. SAM shrugs.)

CHRIS: That was a pretty nice thing you did there.

SAM: Yeah, well . . .

CHRIS: No, really. Good job.

(SAM smiles, pleased.)

Hey, I'm gonna hit the deli. Wanna coffee?

SAM: You bought coffee last time.

CHRIS: Yeah, but the time before that, you bought me a coffee and a doughnut.

SAM: Yeah, but when I lost my wallet—

CHRIS: Dude, let's go down and buy coffee for the people *after* us in line!

SAM; Yes! Chris?

CHRIS: Yeah?

SAM: Good job.

PERSEPHONE

by Jennifer O'Grady

World premiere
Heartland Theatre Company
June 7, 2018
Producing Directors, Rhys Lovell and Gail Dobbins
Normal, Illinois.

Director, Holly Rocke

PERSEPHONE, Kendall Katz
LAURENCE, Cole Cottrell
ELLEN, Jessielee Hinshaw
JILL, Lynda Rettick

Set design, Nick Kilgore
Lighting and sound design, Robert Fulton
Costume design, Clatie Lou Fischer
Props design, Liz Gros
Stage manager, Kayla Russell

CHARACTERS

PERSEPHONE, Thirties. Deceased.
LAURENCE, Thirties. Her husband.
ELLEN, Thirties. Her friend.
JILL, Sixties. Her mother.

SETTING AND TIME

A suburb. The present.

SETS

The play requires a bench that, with cushions, could double as a sofa, as well as a chair and a small table.

PERSEPHONE in light. She speaks to the audience.

PERSEPHONE: I remember this one day. Everything froze over. There was ice everywhere, and not slushy ice but the kind you can't see, that sends you careening on your backside. There was a pile-up and the EMTs couldn't make it. Laurence had to carry me. That was nice. But not for him. You know what? I'm talking too much. Look.

(*LAURENCE in a spot. He can't see PERSEPHONE. He is crouched, as if speaking to a small child.*)

LAURENCE: I know it seems weird. But Mommy isn't in that box. She's not in her body anymore.

PERSEPHONE: (*To audience.*) An instant diet. Ha!

LAURENCE: We don't really know where she is. She's somewhere nice. But it's just for her.

PERSEPHONE: (*To audience.*) I'm dead, by the way.

LAURENCE: No. They have their own rules there. But you have Mommy right here.

(*Points to his head.*)

That means you get to carry her around with you. Forever.

PERSEPHONE: Sort of.

LAURENCE: Let's go get ice cream.

(*He stands. PERSEPHONE goes very close to him. He looks around a little, perhaps sensing something, but no one is there. A beat. He exits.*)

PERSEPHONE: (*To audience.*) Seph is what he calls me. No one else calls me that. Mother taught classics. "Persephone," what was she thinking? She made my life a parade of bad jokes. "Hey, it's Perse-PHONEY! Ha ha!" "Well, well, Persephone. Does that mean you'll go underground half the year?" When I met Laurence it wasn't like that. He asked me my name, and I expected the stare. He said: "Persephone. Would you like a drink?" I was sick a long time. One day I couldn't breathe. Laurence carried me out. Now I'm here. Laurence has a business, I mean he works all the time. I did everything for Sam. He's three. I had a mommy. Laurence had a mommy. Everyone at Sam's little school has a mommy. No one should grow up without a mommy. (*Beat.*) I'm going to get him one.

(*A library. ELLEN at a table with books. PERSEPHONE approaches, but ELLEN can't see her.*)

PERSEPHONE: (*To audience.*) That's my friend, the librarian. I met Ellen at school. We each got married, then moved back here. One day Ellen came home early from work and found her husband and some floozy going at it in bed. Ellen packed her bags, then came to me.

(*Lights change: a flashback. ELLEN cries softly. PERSEPHONE holds her hand.*)

ELLEN: Am I too skinny? Are my clothes boring? She had red high heels for Christ's sake . . .

PERSEPHONE: Nothing's wrong with you, El. It's him.

ELLEN: We were going to buy a house . . .

PERSEPHONE: Good thing you didn't. Face it, men are dicks.

ELLEN: Not Laurence.

PERSEPHONE: I got lucky. But people change. We age, we lose our minds. Tom's afraid. We all are.

(*To audience.*)

Ellen knew I was sick.

ELLEN: I'm so sorry, Persephone. Here I am going on about myself, when . . .

PERSEPHONE: Forget it. You have a right to be happy. Without him.

ELLEN: I found an apartment on Anchor Street. With bay windows.

PERSEPHONE: That's great. We'll have a party. Listen, I have to pick up Sam now. I'll be back, okay?

(Lights change back: the present. ELLEN handles the books. To audience:)

Now she's alone. Says she likes her life.

(She gives us a long look.)

I hope she still likes kids. Guess I'd better find out.

(A bookstore window. PERSEPHONE waits. ELLEN enters and begins to cross. PERSEPHONE goes in front of her and blows in her face. ELLEN stops, then waves the air as if she just walked into a swarm of gnats. PERSEPHONE continues to blow, ELLEN continues to wave. In this way PERSPHONE turns ELLEN around, so that ELLEN faces the bookstore window. PERSEPHONE stops blowing. ELLEN sees something in the window.)

ELLEN: Oh. . .

(She goes into the store.)

PERSEPHONE: (*To audience.*) See? We can do things.

(ELLEN emerges with a shopping bag. She takes out her cellphone and dials.)

ELLEN: Laurence? Hi, it's Ellen. I just saw something that might be good for Sam. Could I bring it over? . . Eight o'clock. Sure. See you then.

(She hangs up and then exits.)

PERSEPHONE: (*To audience.*) Eight o'clock. I can't wait.

(LAURENCE's living room. Shortly before eight. LAURENCE, dressed neatly, sits on a couch. PERSEPHONE sits in a chair, staring at LAURENCE, who can't see her. Sound of a doorbell. He stands, and then exits.)

LAURENCE: (*Offstage.*) Mother. How are you?

PERSEPHONE: Damn.

JILL: (*Offstage.*) Not well, Laurence.

(*He re-enters with JILL. JILL wears a pantsuit.*)

JILL: The book club ran late again, but I was hoping I could see Sam. Is he asleep?

LAURENCE: I'm afraid so. Something to drink?

JILL: I'll help you.

(*LAURENCE and JILL go off.*)

PERSEPHONE: (*To audience.*) That's my mother. He has to call her Mother. I never called his mother Mother. I have my own mother. One is enough.

(*LAURENCE and JILL re-enter.*)

JILL: When are you going to get decaf, Laurence?

LAURENCE: Sorry, Mother.

JILL: How are you?

LAURENCE: I get by. For Sam's sake.

JILL: How is my little darling?

LAURENCE: I'm not sure. He doesn't really understand.

JILL: It's been seven months, Laurence.

(*Eyeing his clothes.*)

All dressed up tonight, are we?

LAURENCE: I'm expecting a friend. Actually, she's Seph's friend. You know Ellen.

JILL: The one whose husband left her?

LAURENCE: I believe she left him, Mother.

JILL: What difference does it make?

LAURENCE: She's bringing something for Sam.

JILL: That's how it begins.

LAURENCE: How what begins, Mother?

JILL: She doesn't have children of her own, and you're a catch.

(Sound of a doorbell. Pause.)

LAURENCE: That would be Ellen.

JILL: Don't mind me. I'll just wait.

(She goes to the chair, and then changes her mind and sits on the sofa. Beat. LAURENCE looks at her and then exits. PERSEPHONE looks at JILL.)

LAURENCE: (*Offstage.*) Ellen. How are you?

ELLEN: (*Offstage.*) I should be asking you that.

(As LAURENCE and ELLEN converse offstage, PERSEPHONE goes behind JILL and blows on her neck. JILL hunches, as if there's a draft. PERSEPHONE blows some more. JILL shivers, and then goes to the chair and sits. PERSEPHONE sits on the sofa. She examines it, brushing away crumbs.)

LAURENCE: (*Offstage.*) Let me take your coat.

ELLEN: (*Offstage.*) I really can't stay.

LAURENCE: (*Offstage.*) Come in. Just for a moment.

ELLEN: (*Offstage.*) Well, maybe a moment.

(She enters with the shopping bag. LAURENCE follows.)

Jill. How are you?

JILL: Oh, I'm managing. How's. . .the library?

ELLEN: Great. We're building a new wing, a children's wing.

PERSEPHONE: (*To audience.*) She's looking forward to it. Hot dog!

LAURENCE: Have a seat, Ellen.

PERSEPHONE: (*Jumping up.*) Here! Sit here!

(JILL begins to rise but isn't quick enough. ELLEN sits on the sofa. LAURENCE sits besides her. ELLEN takes the book from the bag.)

ELLEN: I hope you like it. I thought it might help.

LAURENCE: (*Takes it and reads.*) *When Mommy Goes to Live in Heaven.*

JILL: Pardon me?

ELLEN: I knew you were having trouble making Sam understand, and . . .

JILL: Persephone was an atheist.

ELLEN: I know, but . . .

JILL: (*To LAURENCE.*) Surely you don't want to fill his head with that nonsense?

LAURENCE: Seph and I always believed he should choose.

JILL: Let me see it, please.

 (*Beat. LAURENCE gives the book to JILL. She opens it, and then reads.*)

JILL: (*Reading.*) "When Mommy goes to Heaven, angels and heavenly beings surround her with light. She will always be happy and never feel pain." Good God, Laurence.

LAURENCE: What? That sounds nice.

JILL: (*Reading.*) "Whenever you say your prayers, you can talk to Mommy. Mommy can't answer you, that's not how it works in Heaven." Oh for Pete's sake.

ELLEN: I'm sorry, I . . .

LAURENCE: No. It's a great book, Ellen.

JILL: Next you'll have him begging for church. How would you like a son who wants to be a monk?

LAURENCE: He's three, Jill. All he wants is to play with trucks.

ELLEN: Maybe I should go.

LAURENCE: No!

JILL: Stay, Ellen. I know when I'm not wanted.

LAURENCE: Mother, please . . .

JILL: Don't bother. I'll let myself out.

PERSEPHONE: Good.

(JILL exits. A silence.)

ELLEN: I should . . .

LAURENCE: No. (*Beat.*) I mean . . . usually it's just me. But if you have to be somewhere . . .

ELLEN: I can stay.

LAURENCE: Don't mind Jill. What I think is, she used to have all these myths, you know? Then her husband dies. Then her—only child . . . What does she have now but stories? I think she hates all that now, and when you hate what you loved . . .

ELLEN: It's okay.

LAURENCE: I really like this book, El. I'll read it to Sam tomorrow.

(He sees that ELLEN is smiling.)

Did I—say something . . . stupid?

ELLEN: Persephone was the only one who ever called me El. It's nice to be El again.

(Pause. She stands, and then LAURENCE stands.)

LAURENCE: I'll walk you to the door.

(They exit. PERSEPHONE doesn't move. Offstage.)

Bye, El. Thanks again.

(He re-enters, then picks up the book. He looks at it, and then exits.)

PERSEPHONE: (*To audience.*) Okay. This is what I wanted. (*Pause.*) One more thing to do. Let there be light.

(JILL in her house, trying to read. A dead plant sits on a table. JILL, unable to concentrate, closes the book. She leans back and closes her eyes. PERSEPHONE enters with a plant, the same kind as the dead one, but very much alive.)

PERSEPHONE:(*To audience.*) Shh. It won't work if she sees. She'll just freak out. She needs something to believe in.

(*She replaces the dead plant with the living one.*)

When I was kid I asked her about my name. She said, "You should feel lucky. I have the name of a nursery-rhyme character, and you're a goddess." But I never chose to be a goddess. I never asked for that.

(*She looks at JILL, and then exits with dead plant. Sound of a slammed door. JILL wakes with a start and sees the living plant. She goes to it, and touches it.*)

JILL: My God.

(*Blackout. PERSEPHONE in light.*)

PERSEPHONE: (*To audience.*) They've had dinner a few times. Last night it was French. Ellen wore her green dress. Usually it means something, when she wears that dress. Laurence wore his purple shirt, the one he never touched. I'd say, "Honey, why don't you ever wear that shirt?" He'd say it was too good for just anything. They took El to the aquarium. They looked at all the turtles. Sam asked if the turtles were sad, and she said, "Why should they be sad? They get to look at you." Sam took her to school. She got to see his paintings, his little chair. Maybe when you're dead, you can't feel happy. You can feel peaceful. You can feel no pain. Maybe you can't feel happy. (*Pause.*) They're going to the park tomorrow. This could be it.

(*A park bench, on which LAURENCE and ELLEN sit. PERSEPHONE watches them. ELLEN is taking things out of a paper bag.*)

ELLEN: So there's this.

(*She takes out a plastic-wrapped black-and-white cookie.*)

LAURENCE: Mmm. Nice plastic.

ELLEN: And this.

(*Takes out a giant Santa-head lollipop.*)

LAURENCE: It's July.

ELLEN: It was discounted. And this.

(Takes out a water pistol.)

LAURENCE: I love those.

ELLEN: It's for Sam. But if you're nice, you can share.

(He smiles.)

I told you I'd surprise you. I always liked that weird store.

LAURENCE: (*Looks out toward audience.*) Look at him on that slide. For months I thought he'd never leave my side.

ELLEN: (*Looking.*) Look. He made a friend.

(He looks at her. A beat. He looks away.)

What?

LAURENCE: It isn't fair to you, Ellen.

ELLEN: What isn't?

LAURENCE: Everyone else gets up and goes on. Another day. And each day moves farther away from *that* day, the day she died. But I don't move. It's always that day in my head, and I think . . . what could I have done? What didn't I do?

ELLEN: Laurence, if Persephone knew you blamed yourself, it would break her heart. It's all right. You need to cry.

(They hold each other. He looks at her, and then moves as if to kiss her. Then LAURENCE and ELLEN suddenly go dark. Pause.)

PERSEPHONE: (*To Audience.*) Love isn't saying or feeling. It's doing. Even when nobody knows what you've done. When no one will ever know. A heart carved in a forest. A flag up on a mountain peak. Do ghosts cry? I'm about to find out.

(Lights fade.)

THE POLE AT THE CENTER

by C.S. Hanson

Performed by
The Bechdel Group
Studio Lab at the Drama Guild
24-Hour Writing Challenge
January 29, 2018
New York City

Produced as thanks for the donors of the 2017 Write for Women Campaign.

JANET, Polly Adams
SHARON, Barbara Matovu
MONIQUE, Stacy Renae.
DAKOTA, Zena Hinds
OLIVE, Sarah Teed

Producer, Gina L. Grandi

CHARACTERS

JANET, 50, female, a patron of the arts.
SHARON, 40, female, public school art teacher.
MONIQUE, 15, female, student.
DAKOTA, 15, female or transgender, student.
OLIVE, 15, female, student.

TIME

Present day.

SETTING

The art room in a public school in an urban city. It's not fancy. Works of art created by students hang on the walls. A podium has been set up for a presentation.

COSTUMES

Janet is dressed professionally in a suit appropriate to a day on Wall Street. Sharon is wearing a party dress. The teenagers are dressed casually in what they wore to school that day.

Lights up on the art room in a public school. A "Thank You to Our Donors" sign isn't professional, but it does the job. JANET enters and SHARON rushes to her.)

SHARON: Oh my goodness, Janet, is it you?

JANET: Of course it is. Hello, Sharon.

SHARON: The students will be so excited. You're like royalty around here.

JANET: Oh please.

SHARON: My principal is finally taking me seriously. He can't believe I actually set this all in motion. Thank you, Janet! Thank you so—

JANET: It was a small contribution. The room looks lovely.

SHARON: Used to be the supply room. Rolls of toilet paper stacked to the ceiling. This school district has more toilet paper than—oh, sorry. You have no idea what you have done for—

JANET: Honestly, I don't want any attention. By the way, who are all these people?

SHARON: When I told the principal you were coming, he invited the school board, and then the arts committee. Then some community arts advocates heard about it, and oh, gosh, there's a member of the press right here, in this room.

JANET: Uh, I really can't stay. I have a car waiting. I just wanted to say congratulations in person.

SHARON: You have to stay. We planned a ceremony.

JANET: Ceremony? I don't have to say anything, do I?

SHARON: You must do this sort of thing all the time.

JANET: Sharon, I'm happy to have contributed to the arts program, but no, I don't go around making speeches. And I usually donate anonymously.

SHARON: Please, for the students? Three of my most gifted—I call them my little angels—they're going to unveil an art project they worked on for the opening. Janet, this is the first dedicated "arts room" in the history of P.S. 116. Thanks to you, we have more funding than the track team.

JANET: Well, I like the fact that you're putting the students' art works on display.

SHARON: Makes them feel like real artists. That's what happens. They start acting and behaving like artists. Oh, there they are.

(MONIQUE, DAKOTA, and OLIVE enter, wheeling in a large canvas covered in a sheet of cloth.)

JANET: You know, Sharon, I'm not the hero in this. You are. You wrote to me. You got me to visit.

SHARON: This isn't about me—although I did splurge on a new dress for the occasion.

JANET: Okay, I know what I'm going to tell this crowd.

SHARON: If anything, talk about the students. Make them feel special.

(To the students.)

Monique? Come. Olive? Dakota? Come and meet—

(The students approach.)

MONIQUE: Whoa. It's you. The Janet.

SHARON: Monique, we address her as Ms. Vanderworth.

JANET: Call me Janet.

DAKOTA: Okay, Janet. I didn't think you were real.

SHARON: Dakota, you know she's real. And this is Olive.

(*They all shake hands with JANET.*)

JANET: I am very honored to meet you all.

OLIVE: We are so honored. I mean, I could cry, what you've done.

JANET: Sharon tells me you're the most promising art students at the school.

DAKOTA: Not really. We just like to mess around.

SHARON: Okay, it's time. Get ready for the unveiling—I'll prompt you—and then Janet will say a few words.

MONIQUE: Mrs. Greenburg, we can't stay.

(*The students try to leave.*)

SHARON: You can't leave. You're the artists. This is all about you.

OLIVE: We can't stay. Believe me.

DAKOTA: She means it's not ready. Really.

MONIQUE: See you tomorrow, Mrs. Greenburg.

(*They start to haul the canvas out of the room.*)

SHARON: You are staying. You can leave after the ceremony.

(*She goes to the podium.*)

Ladies and gentlemen. I'm Sharon Greenburg, head of the art department here at P.S. 116. Thank you all for being here. Thank you for believing in arts education. I want you to know, we have a super hero among us . . . I'm talking about Janet Vanderworth. Thanks to Janet, we now have a dedicated arts room. Look around. Art created by our students in every corner. It's a real gallery of art. Now, please, everyone, let us raise a toast to Janet, as we unveil the newest work of art from Monique, Dakota, and Olive, who made something special for this occasion.

(*The students try to slip out.*)

Get back here. Suddenly they are so shy.

(She physically brings the students back to the front of the room.)

I am told this is a mixed media project with a focus on photorealism. Now, let's see if we can coordinate this. As we raise our glasses in a toast to Janet Vanderworth . . . the students will unveil—oh, and Janet, come up here.

(JANET comes to the front of the room.)

Okay, everyone, glasses? Now, the unveiling.

(The students don't budge.)

Oh goodness, I'll do it myself. Here's to Janet.

(She unveils a larger-than-life photorealistic painting. A bold title runs up the side: THE JANET. Central to the piece is a scantily clad stripper on a pole. It is a blown-up photo of Janet at a younger age. There are gasps throughout the room.)

No. No. No. What is the meaning of this? What did you devils do?

OLIVE: I'm sorry. I'm sorry. We shouldn't have.

DAKOTA: Told you we're not done.

JANET: Where did you find—

SHARON: Done. You're done. You are expelled. All three of you. This is— oh, Janet, I'm so sorry. Everyone, I am so sorry. This is my fault. I should have seen it in advance.

(To the girls.)

I trusted you.

JANET: Are you trying to ruin me?

SHARON: Well it's not you, Janet.

JANET: That photo—where did you find—?

DAKOTA: You can find anything on the Internet.

SHARON: Janet, we all know that's not you on that POLE! That is a fake, vulgar, repulsive, irresponsible—. Cover it up.

OLIVE: I'm really sorry.

(She tries to cover up the canvas.)

MONIQUE: Olive, what's your problem? You were part of it.

OLIVE: I know but, Janet's a real person. She seems nice.

SHARON: That is not Janet.

JANET: It is me.

SHARON: No it's not.

DAKOTA: See? It's her.

JANET: Why would you do this?

DAKOTA: We were exploring. Like the teacher tells us to do

SHARON: "The teacher?" now I'm just "the teacher? And that's not what I meant by exploring.

OLIVE: We didn't mean anything.

JANET: You didn't mean anything? Art means something. What you create better mean something, or what are we doing here?

OLIVE: I, um, painted that halo to shine a light on the truth.

JANET: And how would you know the truth of that picture?

DAKOTA: It means shining a light on the one percent.

SHARON: This event is over. Everything's over.

JANET: You think this represents the one percent? This represents the best business model I could find for putting myself through college and business school. It represents hard work and a few disgusting moments, and also a certain physical joy in working that pole.

MONIQUE: She likes it.

SHARON: She doesn't like it.

JANET: What does it matter whether I like it? I might have been born into privilege, but it all went sour because of art.

SHARON: Don't you have a car waiting?

JANET: Yes, I have a car waiting. But I want to say something before this hits the tabloids.

SHARON: Please, no, no press.

JANET: My mother made art. And she was ostracized by her family for her art. She put cow dung on the Madonna or something like that.

SHARON: There is no reason for explanations.

JANET: Oh really? Well, you're probably all wondering if I was a prostitute.

SHARON: Nobody's wondering about that, Janet.

JANET: Of course, they're wondering. Look at that woman on that pole. No, I wasn't. I was an exotic dancer, a stripper.

SHARON: I think we can just cover it up now.

JANET: Leave it. It was a job. My mother's artwork was so controversial, she was cut off in every way imaginable—emotionally, financially. I was nine years old. My world came apart.

SHARON: We owe you an apology.

JANET: What good would that do? It's too late.

OLIVE: We didn't mean to hurt you.

JANET: I guess it's rather courageous of you. Even creative.

SHARON: Oh you don't have to praise it.

JANET: I'm looking at something I thought I'd never see again. I'm a banker. And a supporter of causes. But I guess I won't be running for president.

DAKOTA: You should. You're smart. You been through a lot.

JANET: Maybe you should, Dakota. But why would I vote for you?

DAKOTA: 'Cuz I represent change. Just like you. And you inspired something in us. It's like, we brought our world into the photo. It's not just you anymore. It's our hardships. Things I find on the street.

MONIQUE: And the thing with the cash? The dollars floating in from above and below and the sides? It's like—I don't know, the dancer, she's got everything. You got money coming at you, that's power. And the pole is the center. I'm not explaining it right.

OLIVE: We lead the viewer up and down that pole. The pole steadies the entire composition.

DAKOTA: First it was like, I just wanted to wake everyone up. I'll be honest, I was like, I was jealous. Mrs. Greenburg, all you talked about was Janet this and Janet that. She doesn't know our world. And then I found this picture. And I knew it was her.

MONIQUE: And that pole was golden.

OLIVE: We started and we couldn't stop.

DAKOTA: You tell us to be bold, Mrs. Greenburg, we are bold. And we get picked on for being the art geeks.

MONIQUE: Yeah, we get picked on, and I'm gonna start smacking some of those people around.

OLIVE: We're getting stronger. Our art is saying something. I think it's a symbol of strength, the pole.

DAKOTA: But I kind of forgot THE JANET was a real person.

OLIVE: It's not just you on that pole. It's a lot of things. It's survival.

MONIQUE: Or something.

JANET: Survival. Yes. You got it.

SHARON: I really am sorry.

JANET: I'm not. No one should be punished for the freedom to create art. I will continue funding this effort as long as you keep encouraging students to be brave. My message to you? Never stop. Never ever shut down.

SHARON: Oh, Janet!

OLIVE: Thank you.

(The students gleam. So does JANET.)

JANET: Now I have to go home and tell my family how their mom got her education before she became a hot shot on Wall Street.

STALLED

by Sharon E. Cooper

Stalled was developed with the The CRY HAVOC Workshop (www.cry havoccompany.org) and further developed in the Stillwater Writer's Group. A staged reading of *Stalled* was in The Future is Female festival in New York City in 2017. It was directed by Jessica Bauman and featured Bianca Leigh and Nina Mehta.

World premiere
Samuel French Off-Off Broadway Play Festival
Vineyard Theatre
August 2018
New York City

Director, Jessica Bauman
Actors, Ali Lawrence and Bianca Leigh
Wardrobe designer, Flavia Colucci
Photographer, Mikaela Martin

CHARACTERS

SARAH, late 40s.
DESEREE, late 40s.

NOTE

DESEREE is a transgender woman. If you need to adjust the characters' ages in either direction in order to cast a transgender actor to play DESEREE, please do so. SARAH and DESEREE can be any racial or ethnic background.

TIME

New Year's Eve, just before midnight, the present.

SETTING

A nice hotel bathroom in a small town. This play can easily accommodate various budgets. For example, chairs could represent the stalls and a table could represent the bathroom counter.

The playwright would like to thank all involved in the development of the piece, especially Jessica Bauman and Bianca Leigh, as well as Delia M. Kropp, who provided tremendous resource to the playwright.

A row of bathroom stalls. Flashy heels, belonging to DESEREE, hang below the stall and a pair of plain black pumps in the stall next to hers shift slightly from side to side. They belong to SARAH. We can't see either woman. Just their feet. The sound of a toilet flushing.

SARAH: Could you pass me some toilet paper?

DESEREE: Sure.

SARAH: There isn't enough in here.

> (*Hands reach under the stalls. Toilet paper is exchanged. The sounds of sniffling from under one of the doors.*)

I'm gonna need more than this!

DESEREE: Okay!

> (*SARAH reaches under the stall. DESEREE throws an entire roll of toilet paper over the top of the stall. SARAH catches it. DESEREE steps out of the stall in a fashionable red dress. She heads for the sink and starts washing her hands. SARAH opens the stall; her sailor dress (or some equivalent that says she's trying and failing at looking cool) hangs on her*

boxy body. Her zipper is stuck in the back. She's holding back tears as she steps out and tries, unsuccessfully, to zip up her dress, getting caught up in her sweater. DESEREE reapplies red lipstick and watches Sarah in the mirror. DESEREE recognizes SARAH as SARAH washes her hands.)

DESEREE: So—*Hi!*—Happy New Year.

SARAH: Yeah, Happy New Year. I like your skinny heels.

(DESEREE hands her a paper towel. SARAH pats her face and blows her nose into the paper towel.)

DESEREE: Oh—thanks.

SARAH: I would wear something like that if I didn't have plantar fasciitis or high heel-itis. It's a real thing, high heel-itis. If I put it on the Internet, it'd be a real thing. Anything anyone puts on the Internet is a real thing, right?

(She notices DESEREE staring at her.)

Do I have spinach in my hair? I was eating it earlier and that's—

DESEREE: No—no, you don't. God—uh—

SARAH: Sorry, I'm a little—at midnight my husband's getting married.

DESEREE: Your *husband.*

(During the following, SARAH returns to trying to fix her zipper. The zipper is winning.)

SARAH: When you say something for sixteen years, it's hard to stop. It's like if you woke up one day and you were in an elevator with strangers and you couldn't say, "Nice weather" or "Bad weather" or basically anything about weather. It's programmed, saying "My husband." It's just that it's not true anymore. Could you help me with this?

(She indicates the zipper. DESEREE tries to help.)

DESEREE: So—why are you *here*—at your ex-husband's wedding?

SARAH: My daughter wanted me to come. She wanted all of us to be together, a big, happy—The invitation said, "Ring in the New Year; celebrate our new life." So every year from now on when I hear the countdown, I'll be like, "Oh great, it's the anniversary of when I was in the bathroom when my ex-husband got married!"

DESEREE: I can see why—

(She continues to work on the zipper.)

SARAH: "Celebrate *our* new *life*." Is that even grammatically correct? Shouldn't it be our new *lives*. Or is it supposed to be like—oh we are now one, bound—forever—like Jesus on the cross.

(Looking up.)

Sorry Jesus.

DESEREE: Your zipper is stuck.

SARAH: (*Snappy.*) Yes, thank you, I know. (*Softer.*) Sorry. Maybe it's a sign I shouldn't go.

DESEREE: Where's your daughter?

SARAH: Somewhere out there. They're getting married in ten minutes, right after the countdown.

DESEREE: I know. I'm sorry about Steve.

(SARAH takes a good look at DESEREE.)

SARAH: Are you Robert's mom? From the PTA?

DESEREE: No.

SARAH: Do you work over at the bakery on—

DESEREE: No.

SARAH: Neighbor?

(DESEREE shakes her head no.)

Doctor?

(DESEREE shakes her head no.)

Sorry, I'm terrible at faces.

DESEREE: Do you have a pencil?

SARAH: You work in a pencil—place?

DESEREE: For your zipper.

SARAH: Ooohhhh.

(She digs in her bag and hands her a pencil. She hands it to DESEREE, turns around and—)

I really don't understand how a pencil—I mean, what are you going to do—erase my—

DESEREE: (*Overlapping completely.*) Let's—see. Let me—just—this might—voila!

SARAH: What?! You are a miracle worker.

DESEREE: Maybe it's a sign you should go—

(Looking at SARAH's splotchy face.)

—but you could use a little—

(She reaches in her bag and takes out some blush. She places it on SARAH.)

My Mama says a little blush and the right lipstick could make a rainbow out of a rainy day. There . . . that's nice . . . do you have any lipstick?

SARAH: Sorry, who are you again?

DESEREE: I'm Deseree. Formerly known as Derek. Kind of like you were formerly known as being married to Steve. And you are terrible at faces, apparently—

SARAH: Shut the front door! Derek? *Seriously?* Derek?

DESEREE: I was Derek, yes.

SARAH: Yeah! Well, hello! Wow! God, I—Dere—Deser—I—

DESEREE: I know, it's weird—running into your old friend at your ex-husband's wedding and now *he's* a *she.*

SARAH: No—this isn't—weird—this is—normal. Totally normal. I'm really comfortable. Is there any water in here?

(DESEREE points at the sink. SARA slurps water into her mouth.)

DESEREE: I was surprised by the invitation. It seems like he invited the whole debate team.

SARAH: Wait. So when did you—

DESEREE: It's been a process. A long process.

SARAH: Well, you—look—great, better than me, and I've always been a—

(*Looking at DESEREE.*)

DESEREE: You've always been a what?

SARAH: I've always been a—*person* who liked you.

DESEREE: That's true. You had a crush on me.

SARAH: I did not.

DESEREE: You totally did.

SARAH: Everyone had a crush on you.

DESEREE: Senior year. We sat together in the soundproof courtyard for lunch every day and when Mrs. Nickels walked by, we'd smile and wave and yell, "Hi Mrs. Nipples!" And she'd wave—and we'd laugh.

SARAH: She did have huge breasts.

DESEREE: And you ate one tub of French fries and two rolls every single day—

SARAH: I'm much healthier now. Remember, I asked you if there was spinach in my hair because I ate it earlier. See, I eat lots of healthy, health foods.

(*Touching some part of her body.*)

I still have a little extra weight, you know, from my daughter, Eliza.

DESEREE: How old is she?

SARAH: Three—teen.

DESEREE: Three—teen? Thirteen?

SARAH: You say potato and I—I like potatoes. Okay, fine, I still *love potatoes*. But *you*—you were perfect at everything: student council president, you let me cheat in AP Bio, you were the best parallel parker. The first time I let Eliza drive, I thought I was going to have a heart attack.

DESEREE: You let your thirteen-year-old drive?

SARAH: Okay. She's sixteen. Sixteen plus one. Seventeen. She's seventeen okay? Stop pressuring me.

DESEREE: (*Calmly.*) I—wasn't—

SARAH: I *wish* she were thirteen. Or three. Or any age going backwards instead of forwards. At three, she'd scream about not having another cookie or another cartoon and I wanted to run out of the room. I wanted to run out of the house. Now it's Snapchat and late-night parties and only living with me part time until she's in college, when she won't live with me at all, and now I'd do anything to go back to cookies and cartoons. Because there were more years ahead than behind. Because even though it was really hard, I was a part of a team.

> (*DESEREE reaches out and touches SARAH's shoulder. A moment.*)

DESEREE: If a man, a woman, and a kid were the only definition of a family, hardly anyone would be in one. I mean, outside of this town. And this town sucks.

SARAH: I still live here.

DESEREE: Right. What I meant was that your daughter—she'll always be your daughter. You'll always be her mom. Soon, she'll be bringing home laundry and boyfriends and—

SARAH: She likes girls.

DESEREE: Oohhh . . . .

SARAH: That's what she told me last year over s'mores.

DESEREE: How did that go?

SARAH: I brought out a bottle of champagne and she pretended that she hadn't had champagne before. And I toasted her and pretended that I was okay with her liking girls. It took me a little bit of time to be okay with it, I still—

> (*Looking at DESEREE.*)

—I thought it was more important to pretend than to make her feel like there was anything wrong with her.

DESEREE: I wish my family had pretended. My dad told his friends I died and my mom didn't say anything.

(They stand for a moment and say nothing.)

SARAH: Why didn't you call me?

DESEREE: It was Steve's wedding, and I didn't think you'd be here.

SARAH: I meant why didn't you call me *ever*? I don't know—I would have—I think I could have—I thought we were friends. And then, one day, I never heard from you ever again.

DESEREE: I had to take that time.

SARAH: (*About DESEREE but also about Steve.*) People shouldn't quit on each other.

DESEREE: I—I needed to build—something—somewhere else—that had nothing to do with this shithole. No offense.

SARAH: No—none taken—

DESEREE: (*Overlapping.*) To make my life that you thought was so perfect actually be okay. For me. I haven't been back much. It took a long—a long time for things to be better with my mom. After my dad died a few years ago, I felt like I could finally breathe. During the funeral, I stood next to my Mama, and the pastor kept saying he was a great family man. Later at home, Mama pulled me in her room and I thought we were going to have a "talk" and she handed me a little bag with half a dozen shades of red lipstick and said, "Girl, you look good. But you should wear more red" and I was like—"It's a funeral." And we laughed.

SARAH: You do look good in red.

DESEREE: Yes, I do.

SARAH: So why did you decide to come here, now for—

DESEREE: I—I didn't want to make this wedding about me; I don't want to make this about me. It's just—I got this invitation and I called Steve and he was actually pretty nice—he said, "Come anyway."

SARAH: Yeah, that Steve, he's a nice guy . . . Have you seen him?

DESEREE: For the last half hour, I've been stalling in the car, watching people I haven't seen in years walking by. I finally got up my nerve, looked at my reflection in the mirror, and heard my Mama's voice: "Girl, you look good." But then I went to pick up my place card and it said "Derek." And it hit me. Steve probably told some people. Over the years, I've run into some people. Does everyone know? Is everyone going to be gawking at me or whispering behind my back like I'm some kind of specimen? Are people going to be more interested to talk *about* Derek vs. Deseree instead of just talking to me? So I turned around and was going to walk right back out the door but instead I walked into this bathroom. The one with the lady in a skirt.

(A moment.)

SARAH: Did you ever have children?

DESEREE: No. But I do have a family. The most amazing people.

SARAH: Do you have any pictures?

(DESEREE pulls out her phone.)

DESEREE: Of course.

(Pointing.)

This is Eleanore. She's a real estate agent like me. A real pisser. She outsells me every damn month and makes me laugh every day. Greg and Delilah are my neighbors. They walk my dog when I'm late. This is my dog, Ruffles. She barks a lot. Get it—Ruff-les. Every time I come home, it's like I've just come back from war; she's so happy. Oh, and this is my boyfriend, Allan. He's always traveling for work but he's the nicest damn man I've ever met. To make up for being gone so much, he watches my favorite reality TV shows with me—I mean, really, who can watch the news these days?

(On her phone.)

Look! See, I told you—this

(Laughing.)

This is a picture of us watching TV!

(She notices SARAH, who is both happy for and jealous of DESEREE.)

SARAH: It looks like you have a great family there.

DESEREE: Show me a picture of your daughter.

(SARAH pulls out her phone and shows DESEREE Eliza's picture.)

DESEREE: Oh—she looks like you. Pretty, poised, smart, looks like she has a good sense of humor, just like her mom. I'd like to meet her. Someday.

SARAH: Someday?

(DESEREE points to the time on SARAH's phone.)

DESEREE: If you don't leave soon, you'll miss the wedding. Pretend if you have to, put on a face if you have to, but go sit with your daughter.

SARAH: So, wait, you're not coming?

DESEREE: You should go.

SARAH: I deleted every picture of me and Steve on Facebook. I unfriended him on the day he posted, "She said Yes." And then I updated my status and said, "I'm really happy for Steve" and thirty-seven people liked it. I don't want people to gawk at me, either.

DESEREE: You need—do you have any lipstick in there?

(She leans over and looks in SARAH's large bag. She finds a lipstick and hands it to Sarah. As SARAH applies the lipstick, DESEREE pulls Sarah's hair back into a clip.)

DESEREE: No reason to hide that face . . . . There, now you're ready.

SARAH: What about you?

DESEREE: I didn't promise anyone anything.

(SARAH looks at DESEREE and then herself in the mirror. She looks back at DESEREE and then walks towards the door.)

Happy New Year, Sarah.

(SARAH stops and turns to DESEREE.)

SARAH: Happy New Year, Deseree.

(She leaves. DESEREE looks in the mirror. She pulls out her red her lipstick, applies it—and then, DESEREE leaves, too.

(Blackout)

TRACY AND HER DREAM GUYS

by Michael Higgins

First produced by
Otherworld Theatre
November 17, 2018
2018 Paragon Play Festival
Festival Curator, Elliott Sowards
Chicago, IL

Director, Rory Jobst

TRACY, Nina D'Angier
ACTIVIST / COWBOY, Tim Larson
MOM, Beth Harris

CHARACTERS

TRACY, Female, 20s, an overworked staff member at a wildlife conservation group.
ACTIVIST, Male, 20s/early 30s, an inspiring social activist and TV commentator.
COWBOY, Male, 20s/early 30s, a rugged but gentle cowboy.
MOM, Female, 40s–60s, Tracy's demanding mother.

Actors of any race or ethnicity can play all characters. Diverse casting is recommended.

TIME

Present.

SETTING

The bedroom of TRACY's small apartment, which can be minimally suggested. (During the play, TRACY will dream of being in three other locations: a TV studio, a stretch of open range in the Old West, and her childhood bedroom. But no set change is required.)

Lights up on TRACY, asleep in bed. She is wearing an eye mask, sweatpants, and an oversized Chicago Bulls T-shirt with the "bull's head" logo on the front. On a nightstand by the bed is an alarm clock. ACTIVIST sits in a chair near the bed. He wears a sports coat, an earpiece, and has a lapel mic clipped to his shirt. He talks to the audience, as if speaking into a TV camera.

ACTIVIST: . . . I agree. Americans who struggle in our small towns deserve as much compassion as those who face hardship in our cities. What I object to is the con game.

(TRACY sits up in bed. Groggy, she pulls up her eye mask, which leaves her hair askew.)

—The scam that tells rural America the answer is not fair wages, but union busting. Not strong public education, but shady for-profit colleges.

(As TRACY looks on, admiringly.)

Not affordable health care, but tax cuts for the rich that saddle their children with mountains of debt. The same con game your network runs seven days a week.

(ACTIVIST holds his "serious face" for a beat, then relaxes and looks at TRACY.)

Tracy—how you doing?

TRACY: I didn't mean to interrupt.

ACTIVIST: Nah, you're good. They just went to commercial.

TRACY: I like listening to you.

ACTIVIST: Stick around. We'll hang out.

TRACY: (*Looking at her alarm clock.*) I can't.

ACTIVIST: Are you going in early again?

TRACY: I have to. Work is crazy right now. It's the rhinoceros thing.

ACTIVIST: There's a rhinoceros where you work? You should call building maintenance.

TRACY: No, the rhinos are in Asia. I do wildlife conservation. We need to raise a hundred grand by the end of the month to fight illegal poaching.

ACTIVIST: Ah. Got it.

TRACY: All because people think rhino horns are an aphrodisiac . . . . Wait, you're on TV. Tell 'em. Their horns are made of the same stuff as a fingernail. It won't help with . . . you know.

ACTIVIST: The next show is about terrorism . . . Hell, I can work it in.

TRACY: You're awesome.

ACTIVIST: So you'll stay?

    (*Beat.*)

TRACY: Why not? I can't face my real life right now.

ACTIVIST: You look good tonight.

TRACY: (*Laughs—re: her oversized T-shirt.*) Yeah. I'm a supermodel.

ACTIVIST: I'm serious. You know I love my Bulls.

TRACY: Why can't I meet guys like you when I'm awake?

ACTIVIST: Because you're too busy. Why are you still driving your brother to baseball practice?

TRACY: He's only fifteen. He needs a ride.

ACTIVIST: You've got a serious job. Tell your Mom, "I am done being his chauffeur."

TRACY: I'd feel guilty.

ACTIVIST: Guilty of what?

TRACY: Just . . . guilty. I'm the oldest sibling. It's like a disease.

ACTIVIST: Wait. I'm back on.

(Listens to earpiece, then speaks to audience.)

No. *My* position is tougher. Because I say: Target the actual terrorists. Don't lose focus by labeling an entire religion the enemy. I'm also tougher on people who hack our elections, people who praise foreign dictators and—no, I'm not finished—people who falsely believe rhino horns can give them an erection!

(He takes off his lapel mic and does a "mic drop" into his opposite hand.)

TRACY: I wish I could bring you to my Uncle Ted's. He's always badgering me with his stupid political opinions.

ACTIVIST: Just tell him off.

TRACY: I never know what to say. Besides, Mom would freak.

(imitating MOM)

"Don't offend your Uncle."

ACTIVIST: What about him offending you?

(He takes off his sport coat and starts to unbutton his shirt.)

TRACY: What are you doing?

ACTIVIST: I'm going to do this next one with no shirt. Makes me look more forceful.

TRACY: They let you do that?

ACTIVIST: Yeah. Remember two nights ago?

TRACY: (*Suddenly bashful.*) Right. That was . . . That was a good show.

(ACTIVIST continues unbuttoning his shirt—then stops. He listens to his earpiece.)

ACTIVIST: Hang on. They need me at the rally.

TRACY: What rally?

ACTIVIST: (*Leaving the mic and earpiece on his chair.*) If I'm not back in time, you go on instead.

TRACY: Me? No way.

ACTIVIST: You'll do great.

(*He exits.*)

TRACY: No. Come back. I—I can't.

(*Lights change, suggesting a transition to a new "dream world." COWBOY enters, concerned.*)

COWBOY: You alright there, Little Lady?

TRACY: (*Surprised.*) Oh. Hi . . . Cowboy?

COWBOY: You haven't seen Dastardly Darrell, have ya'?

TRACY: No. Who's that?

COWBOY: He's an outlaw, Darlin'. My number one enemy.

TRACY: Oh.

COWBOY: But I ain't a'scared of him. If I see Darrell, I just look him in the eye and say: "Do your worst."

TRACY: (*Not understanding his cowboy accent.*) Do yer werst?

COWBOY: It's a saying we got out here. Like a challenge. You meet a nay-farious character and you ain't a'scared of him, you say: "*Do yer werst.*"

TRACY: Oh . . . That's a good one.

COWBOY: (*Sitting on the bed next to her.*) So what brings you out on the range, Little Lady?

TRACY: Oh, I'm not on the . . .

(*Looks around and sees an open range in the Old West.*)

. . . whoa.

COWBOY: Me, I think the range at sundown is about the nicest place in the whole dern world. The cattle—just startin' to doze off. The stars—just startin' to come out.

TRACY: (*Looks up and is surprised to see stars.*) So beautiful.

COWBOY: (*Looking at TRACY.*) Yes, indeed.

TRACY: (*Laughs.*) Where do I come up with you guys? Some kind of social activist and now a cowboy?

COWBOY: I don't reckon it's a mystery. You've got a lot of stress: job, family, politics being what it is. Part of you wants to fight back—with the help of a brave champion.

TRACY: The activist.

COWBOY: But another part just wishes you could get away. Find someplace where you'd be appreciated. Loved.

TRACY: Here.

> (*COWBOY starts to rub TRACY's shoulders. She wasn't expecting that, but it's nice.*)

COWBOY: 'Prolly explains why I use terms like "Darlin' " and "Little Lady," which in some other context might seem patronizin' or sexist.

TRACY: I know, right? . . . But I can't stay.

COWBOY: I'd take right good care of you.

TRACY: I'm sure you would, but . . .

COWBOY: And we've got cattle here. I know you love cattle.

TRACY: I do?

COWBOY: You got one right there on your blouse.

TRACY: (*Looks down at the Bulls logo.*) Right. It just . . . It doesn't work that way.

COWBOY: Maybe it could. See, I think you're about the sweetest little wildflower that's ever sprung up in these parts.

> (*TRACY turns toward COWBOY, breaking off the shoulder massage.*)

TRACY: I'm not. I'm a mess. I'm an anxious, stressed-out mess.

> (*Off his confused look.*)

Dastardly Darrell? He comes from me—from my mind.

COWBOY: No, Darrell is from Amarillo.

TRACY: I created this world. All the bad things here come from my fears, my anxieties.

COWBOY: Well, I don't know about that. I just know—

TRACY: (*Grabs the alarm clock.*) This is my number one enemy. When it goes off, you and the range and the stars will be gone. And I'll be back in my real life . . . . Let's just enjoy the time we have.

> (*She turns around and taps her shoulder, inviting him to continue the massage.*)

COWBOY: What if I could fix that fancy clock of yours, so it don't trouble you no more?

TRACY: You can't.

COWBOY: (*Standing to leave.*) I've learned some tricks out on this range, Darlin'. I'll be right back.

TRACY: No. Cowboy . . .

COWBOY: And while I'm gone, maybe think on this: I ain't no psyche-ologist. But if all the bad things in this world come from that little bean of yours? Well, then I reckon all the strong and righteous things—they must be in there somewhere, too.

> (*He exits stage left. A beat, as TRACY ponders his words. A noise. She looks left.*)

TRACY: Cowboy?

> (*Turns stage right, concerned.*)

Dastardly Darrell?

> (*MOM enters from behind her, stage left.*)

MOM: Tracy!

TRACY: Mom?

MOM: What do you think you're doing here?

TRACY: I'm . . . visiting a cowboy. What are *you* doing here?

MOM: Oh, "visiting a cowboy." Wonderful. You need to get to work. And don't forget to pick up your brother. We're all having dinner with Uncle Ted.

TRACY: No. I am not dealing with Uncle Ted today.

MOM: Too busy cavorting with some cowboy?

TRACY: Mom, just get out of here, OK?

MOM: No. It took forever to find you. I had to walk through some big protest.

TRACY: You saw the rally?

MOM: It was awful. Fifty degrees outside. Why should I listen to some man without the sense to put on a shirt?

TRACY: I am not having this conversation.

MOM: Then I had to walk down some dusty trail. "Moo! Moo!" You would not believe what I stepped in.

TRACY: Mom, please. Just go.

MOM: I will go when you stop this nonsense and start behaving like an adult.

TRACY: I don't have to behave like an adult! *I'm asleep!*

MOM: Young Lady, as long as you're under my roof, you will not use that tone of voice.

TRACY: I'm not under your . . .

(*Stage lights change; TRACY looks around and feels sick.*)

. . . Oh no.

MOM: And pick up your clothes. Why did I buy that dresser if you're going to throw everything on the floor?

TRACY: Not my old bedroom.

MOM: And these posters. My God, how many boy bands are there?

(*TRACY buries her head in her pillow and screams.*)

MOM: Scream all you want. It won't help . . . What you need to do, Young Lady, is to start caring about your family—and not those stupid rhinos!

(A beat. TRACY lifts her head from the pillow. She's calm now—and dead serious.)

TRACY: I'm going to behave like an adult.

MOM: It's about time.

TRACY: And adults decide for themselves what's important in their lives. Rhinos are important. Picking up Brandon from practice is not.

MOM: He needs a ride.

TRACY: Someone else can do it.

MOM: You're the oldest.

TRACY: No, you are. And if you can't do it, he can find a friend. And if he has no friends, they've got this crazy new invention. It's called a bus.

MOM: Th-there are homeless people on the bus.

TRACY: I will see Uncle Ted on major holidays—that's it. And if he insults my beliefs, I'll tell him exactly how wrong he is. *And* I'll tell him we've all seen his divorce papers and we know those trips to Thailand were not for "business."

MOM: You are not to mention—

(TRACY throws her eye mask and MOM ducks.)

Ah!

TRACY: Goodbye, Mom.

(She closes her eyes, focuses her mind. Stage lights change again. MOM finds herself exiting the stage, against her will.)

MOM: No. Stop that.

(As she is pulled off stage.)

You say all this now. We'll see what happens when you wake up.

TRACY: Yes, we will.

(She picks up the alarm clock. She stares it down. A beat.)

Do your worst.

(Lights fade.)

THE TROUBLE WITH CASHEWS

by David MacGregor

Original production by
Tipping Point Theatre
June 16–17, 2018
Northville, MI

Director, Dani Cochrane

PAUL, Jeff Miller
TARA, Shauna Hitchcock

CHARACTERS

PAUL, Male, younger brother of TARA, in his 20s-40s.
TARA, Female, older sister of PAUL, in her 20s-40s.

SETTING

A backyard family gathering.

TIME

Present day, the Fourth of July.

PAUL stands, a beer in his hand, staring fixedly at the horizon as he is approached by TARA, who has a glass of wine.

TARA: Hi Paul!

PAUL: Mmm.

TARA: How's my little brother doing?

PAUL: I'm above ground.

TARA: Okay . . . it's great seeing you! I'm really glad you could make it to our Fourth of July party this year.

PAUL: Yeah, well . . . what are you gonna do?

   (TARA looks to see what PAUL is staring at, then back to PAUL.)

TARA: Is something wrong?

   (PAUL nods toward the horizon. TARA turns again.)

What?

PAUL: You can't see it?

TARA: See what?

PAUL: Right over there.

TARA: I don't see anything.

PAUL: Yes, you do. Waves of light are pinging around off your retinas and forming images in your brain. What do you see?

TARA: Aunt Dorothy?

PAUL: Bingo.

TARA: What about her?

PAUL: Just watch her.

TARA: Okay . . . I see an old woman sitting at a table, drinking a glass of wine, and eating some nuts out of a bowl.

PAUL: Is that it?

TARA: Pretty much. Am I missing something?

PAUL: Watch when she goes for a nut.

TARA: Okay. And . . . she just ate a nut.

PAUL: Right.

TARA: What about it?

PAUL: Just . . . look, she's doing it again!

TARA: You're right . . . no denying it . . . she ate another nut.

PAUL: Notice anything?

TARA: I really, really want to say yes, but no.

PAUL: You're not looking closely enough! Watch her!

   (Long beat.)

TARA: She just ate another nut.

PAUL: And?

TARA: Paul, all I see is an elderly woman sipping wine and eating nuts.

PAUL: Oh, for God's sake!

TARA: What?

PAUL: What's in that bowl?

TARA: Nuts!

PAUL: What kind of nuts?

TARA: They're . . . it was a, you know, assorted nuts. They come that way. All kinds of different nuts in a bag. I poured them out of the bag, into the bowl, then put them on that table.

PAUL: Exactly. Now, watch her again.

TARA: *(Peering, confused.)* She's eating them one at a time?

PAUL: No! You don't see what she's doing?

TARA: What? What is she doing?

PAUL: She's only eating the cashews!

TARA: What? That's ridiculous—

(PAUL grabs TARA's elbow and turns her ninety degrees.)

PAUL: Don't let her see you!

(A beat, then PAUL and TARA cautiously look sideways.)

And . . . down goes another cashew.

TARA: Paul . . . would you like me to get you some cashews?

PAUL: That's not the point.

TARA: Then—

PAUL: She's looking this way!

(He and TARA turn away, then back.)

TARA: Then what is the point?

PAUL: You're looking at it.

TARA: Paul, you're worrying me.

PAUL: Assorted nuts. What does that mean?

TARA: It means there's more than one kind of nut.

PAUL: For example?

TARA: For example what?

PAUL: What kinds of nuts?

TARA: Well, peanuts . . . um, almonds. I think I saw some hazelnuts, walnuts, and cashews.

PAUL: And is it just a random assortment? Equal amounts of every nut?

TARA: No, I think it's mostly peanuts.

PAUL: Mostly peanuts. And why would that be?

TARA: Because they're cheaper?

PAUL: And they're cheaper because?

TARA: I don't know . . . because they're easier to grow? People like them less than other kinds of nuts?

PAUL: And off the top of your head, of all the nuts you just mentioned, which kind of nut do people like the most?

(Off her hesitation.)

Go on . . . say it.

TARA: Cashews.

PAUL: Cashews.

TARA: You're saying she's deliberately eating only the most expensive and tastiest nuts.

PAUL: And that's not the worst part.

TARA: It's not?

PAUL: No. The worst part is, she knows what she's doing. That's why she keeps looking around to see if anyone is watching. It would be one thing if she were so out of it that she was only eating the nuts she liked best, you know, like a chimp or something. But she knows what she's doing.

TARA: Paul, I can get you some cashews.

PAUL: It's not about the damned cashews! It's about . . . look, who are the two biggest pricks at this party?

TARA: You're talking about our family!

PAUL: Answer the question.

TARA: Reggie and Stan.

PAUL: Reggie and Stan. Now, what do Reggie and Stan have in common, besides being the biggest pricks in the world?

TARA: They're brothers?

PAUL: And who is their mother?

(They both turn back to look at Aunt Dorothy.)

TARA: She just ate another cashew.

(*PAUL takes a deep breath, trying to pull himself together.*)

PAUL: I'm sorry, Tara. See, this is why I shouldn't come to these family things. I get myself all worked up and . . . you know what? Forget it. Forget I said anything. How are you doing? You look great!

TARA: (*Gaze fixed on Aunt Dorothy.*) Goddammit. She's eating all the fucking cashews!

PAUL: I shouldn't have brought it up.

TARA: What the hell? Who does that?

PAUL: Aunt Dorothy, apparently.

TARA: Would you do that?

PAUL: No.

TARA: And neither would I! I would want other people to have some cashews too!

PAUL: Absolutely.

TARA: (*Long beat as she stares.*) Now she's pushing other nuts out of the way to get at the cashews at the bottom of the bowl. This is unbelievable.

PAUL: Tara, I didn't mean to—

TARA: She's not going to stop. She is going to empty that bowl of cashews.

PAUL: And by this point, she probably doesn't even want any more. Now she's just making sure no one else gets any.

TARA: I feel sick. I feel physically ill. How are we even related to her?

PAUL: Well . . . maybe we're not.

TARA: What do you mean?

PAUL: See, that's what I was standing here thinking . . . just trying to make sense of this. And it finally occurred to me . . . maybe she's a reptoid.

TARA: A what?

PAUL: Reptoid. A shape-shifting reptilian humanoid from the Alpha Draconis star system. They're part of a global conspiracy to destroy humanity.

(Off TARA's look.)

Not that I actually believe that! I mean, I'm just speaking, you know, metaphorically.

TARA: No, I think you're onto something.

PAUL: You do?

TARA: Not that I think Aunt Dorothy is a shape-shifting humanoid from another star system. It's worse than that.

PAUL: Seriously?

TARA: She's not an alien. She's one of us. And what she's doing, her behavior, it's hardwired into us. You know the first thing a baby shark does when it's born? It eats all of its brothers and sisters.

PAUL: Like cashews?

TARA: Exactly like cashews. But as we evolved, human beings gradually lost a lot of that sociopathic, me-first impulse, because we realized we were better off working together and being a community and helping one another.

PAUL: So, you're saying that Aunt Dorothy is some kind of throwback to our primeval, reptilian DNA.

TARA: Right. And it would be okay if it were just her and her kids. We'd just be down some cashews. But there's plenty of people just like her. People who not only want their fair share, they want everyone else's share too. In fact, do you know what we're witnessing here? The end of humanity. The total and complete destruction of human beings as a species.

PAUL: Because of Aunt Dorothy?

TARA: Yes! That instinct That primeval, reptilian, I got mine and screw you attitude? Where does that end in a world where every other country and tin-pot dictator has a nuclear arsenal?

PAUL: I never thought of that . . .

TARA: It's us versus them, Paul! The human humans against the reptile humans. And only one side can win.

PAUL: Well, what should we do? I mean, we have to help our side. We can't just stand here and let this happen!

TARA: And we're not going to let it happen. Because this is war. War between people like us and people like Aunt Dorothy and the spawn of her evil loins.

PAUL: Okay then, let's do this. I've got a plan. First, you distract her with, I don't know, some pictures on your phone or something. Then when she's not looking, I'll grab the bowl of nuts. She won't know what hit her!

(*Off TARA's look.*)

What? You don't think that would work?

TARA: Sure it would work. We could steal those nuts but what does that make us? We'd be just like her! Doing whatever we want simply because we can get away with it.

PAUL: Damn it! You're right. Then what do we do?

TARA: The only thing we can do, because drastic measures are called for.

(*She pulls out her car keys and dangles them in front of PAUL's eyes.*)

PAUL: You're going to run her over with your car?

TARA: No! We're going to the grocery store. You and me. And when we come back, we're going to have two five-pound bags of cashews with us. Enough cashews for everyone!

PAUL: Oh yeah . . . yeah! Of course! That's beautiful! That's exactly how it should be, but . . . cashews aren't cheap.

TARA: Either humanity and the planet are worth fighting for, or they're not. Are you in or out?

PAUL: I'm in! Of course, I'm—she's looking this way!

(*He turns away, but TARA doesn't move.*)

TARA: Let her see me. I want her to see me. And I want her to know that I see her.

(She points two fingers towards her eyes, then in the direction of Aunt Dorothy. Emboldened, PAUL does the same thing.)

TARA: She knows. We know. And she knows we know. Game on.

PAUL: I love you, Tara. You're my favorite sibling.

TARA: I'm your only sibling.

(Waving the keys.)

Now, shall we do our part to save the world with delicious cashew goodness for all?

PAUL: We most definitely shall.

(TARA and PAUL link arms and exit.)

12TH STREET

by David Nice

Produced by
Reading Theater Project, Reading, PA
Schumo Theatre at the Yocum Institute for the Arts
3000 Penn Avenue, West Lawn, PA
February 22–24, 2019

Director, Sean Sassaman

MAN, Lauren White
WOMAN, Amy Young

CHARACTERS

MAN and WOMAN could probably be any age over 30 or so. Also, this play could work with two men or two women.

SETTING AND TIME

Now. A city, a door, a kitchen, a table, someone's house.

MAN: Are you going to let me in?

WOMAN: Who? What?

> *(Evaluating him.)*

Why would I let you in?

MAN: This is where I belong.

WOMAN: I think I would know that.

MAN: This is 12th Street.

WOMAN: Yes, but—

MAN: 1308 12th Street.

WOMAN: Yes, but—

MAN: Please let me in.

WOMAN: I don't *know* you.

MAN: Sure you do.

WOMAN: (*She laughs, then stops.*) I don't. This would be funny except I DON'T KNOW YOU.

MAN: Sure. Okay. 1308 North 12th Street. That's me.

WOMAN: That's so weird. No. *South.* South 12th Street. This is 1308 South 12th Street. I don't know you.

MAN: But 1308 *and* 12th. That combination. You don't recognize me?

WOMAN: You do look . . .

MAN: Familiar?

WOMAN: I do recognize you somehow.

MAN: So . . . you'll let me in.

WOMAN: Let you in? Um, let you in? No.

MAN: You see there's a connection though.

WOMAN: I don't see . . . you mean connected by the same street?

MAN: Yes, the street, the number. More. More.

WOMAN: More? How could there be—

MAN: You'll let me in now?

WOMAN: No, my man will be home at twelve thirty or so. Second shift. I can't—

MAN: Maybe *I'm* your man.

WOMAN: I don't—

MAN: I am. I am your man. 1308 North 12th Street.

WOMAN: South.

MAN: Yes, *South*, 1308 South 12th Street.

(She really evaluates him. It takes a while.)

WOMAN: Come in.

(MAN comes in. They both sit down at the table. She pours him a glass of water. He drinks it quickly.)

You're thirsty.

MAN: I am. I am thirsty.

WOMAN: (*Pause. going along with it?*) Okay. Okay. What the hell. How was work today?

MAN: Same as always.

WOMAN: Good. You're still there. You didn't quit.

MAN: No. Yes, I'm still there. I would never quit work.

WOMAN: Good. We need the money.

MAN: Understood. South 12th seems . . . more relaxed . . . more than usual, I mean.

WOMAN: What makes you say . . . it does seem more laid back. Tonight.

MAN: I'm so glad you're home and . . . awake.

WOMAN: Okay. So . . . Am I not usually awake? In the . . .

MAN: North?

WOMAN: Do I sleep well there?

MAN: You sleep all the time. It makes a man . . .

WOMAN: Thirsty.

MAN: Yes . . . hungry or thirsty.

MAN: It's pretty much the same feeling.

WOMAN: It's hard to tell the difference.

WOMAN: North and South 12th Street. That's probably twenty blocks.

MAN: It's twenty-six blocks, but if you . . . it's less than two miles.

WOMAN: Some would say it's a different world.

   (Beat.)

No answer on that one?

MAN: I'll find out. Will I find out?

WOMAN: (*Slowing down to think.*) The North side.

MAN: But I'm *here* now.

WOMAN: You are, for sure. I let you in.

MAN: We're both awake.

WOMAN: He'll be home though. Same as always. My other, the other . . .

MAN: I never work night shift. I'm free in the evenings.

WOMAN: Are you saying . . .

MAN: North and South . . . a kind of dual . . .	WOMAN . . . we'd have two—we'd be . . .
MAN: . . . existence . . . I think it could work	WOMAN: trying two sets of reality . . .
MAN: and make living . . . better, somehow.	WOMAN: So not really giving up more *real* the current life, but boosting everything?

MAN: That seems to be the plan.

WOMAN: Even though you didn't really have a plan. Much. You just switched one—

MAN: North to South. Yep.

WOMAN: Who would have thought that the solution—

MAN: Exactly . . . just change one small aspect and BAM.

WOMAN: How does this really make a difference? Aren't we just—

MAN: I don't think we're substituting one set of facts for another. It's more like . . . a mash-up.

WOMAN: A mash-up?

MAN: Collision? Blend? I feel completely different already. And we haven't even—

MAN: Agreed.	WOMAN: Talked.
Touched.	Kissed?
I don't expect . . .	Sorry, I don't know why I even . . .
It's not like I'm trying to create some crazy *thing* really. Well, maybe . . .	You're not completely a stranger, but I can't really explain how I know what's going on. But I do.

(There is a moment where both are sizing up the other, taking in everything they've just said to each other. They lean into one another and seem drawn to a real moment of gravity, but just before something happens—WOMAN pours another glass of water quickly. MAN, just as quickly, gulps it down.)

MAN: I will be here. I will come here each evening.

WOMAN: Tuesday through Saturday.

MAN: Yes. South. Tuesday through Saturday. My new neighborhood.

WOMAN: *Your* neighborhood.

MAN: Yes. No?

WOMAN: Hmm. Taking possession so quickly.

MAN: Oh. No. Not mine. I meant . . .

WOMAN: It's all right.

MAN:	WOMAN:
It's not . . . I'm not claiming I feel like it's time to just	
	not fight anything
. . . it's more like *being* claimed.	
How is this happening?	I guess I was waiting for something like this to happen.

(There is silence and they start drawing toward each other again. Gravity. They bring their hands up and together as if they are doing a mirror exercise. There is a slow, a very slow bringing of their heads and lips together. They kiss, still touching only their hands, looking as if they are on opposite sides of a window or mirror.)

WOMAN: Well. You want me to believe this has been some spur of the moment, strange thing. But I've seen you . . . I've seen you coming.

MAN: How?

WOMAN: A couple times this summer . . . saw you drive by this block. Slow.

MAN: You saw me?

WOMAN: We saw each other. Think about it.

MAN: South.

WOMAN: Oh, yes, South.

MAN: See . . . there *has* been a plan.

WOMAN: After that . . .

MAN: Yes?

WOMAN: After that . . .

MAN: You come North?	WOMAN: I come North.

   (Lights fade.)

THE VOICE OF THE PEOPLE

by Cary Pepper

Produced by
Bismarck State College Theatre and the BSC Drama Club
Short Play Festival 2019: What Happened to the American Dream?
Co-sponsored by HumanitiesND and the North Dakota Council on the Arts
May 2019

Director, Trey Zent
Supervising Professor, Dr. Danny Devlin
Technical Director, Dean Bellin

LLOYD BRANSON, Tayler Billings
BARBARA CLARK, Shaylyn Lefor
LEO DORN, Nick Winistorfer
VOTERS, Cianna Carlson, Kylee Gifford, DeAnte Kehr, Marissa Carpenter,
    Stephen Loftesnes
JOHN SMITH, Drew Pengilly

CHARACTERS

LLOYD BRANSON, the newsman on the scene.
BARBARA CLARK, the newswoman providing deep background.
LEO DORN, the neighbor who knows everything.

VOTER 1   The
VOTER 2
VOTER 3
VOTER 4   voice
VOTER 5
VOTER 6   of
VOTER 7
VOTER 8
VOTER 9   the
VOTER 10
VOTER 11
VOTER 12people
JOHN SMITH, his record speaks for itself

The play can be performed by 6 ACTORS (3 MEN, 3 WOMEN, though it really doesn't matter) with lots of hats.

SETTING

Various places represented on a bare stage.

TIME

The Present.

Lights up on newsman LLOYD BRANSON.

LLOYD BRANSON: I'm Lloyd Branson, for Up-To-Date Election Coverage. It's Election Day, and I'm standing outside the polling place of Home Haven USA, a small American town of just under 500 people. Home Haven has very simple election protocols. Anyone who wants to run for office simply has to file a petition of intention, and pay a modest administrative fee. One of its residents, John Smith, has done just that. And that's all he's done. After declaring his candidacy for mayor of Home Haven, and filing the required petition, he hasn't been heard from since. He has no staff, no campaign headquarters, no spokesperson, no platform, no proven experience in public office, no party backing, and no endorsements. He has not made a single speech, attended any community meetings, or held one fundraiser. He has not spoken to the media, and has ignored all requests to be interviewed. Almost nothing is known about Smith. He does not show up on Internet searches, and there is no public record of him. According to his petition of intention, he's fifty years old and was born here in town. As his occupation, he listed "politician," though he lists no public offices held. He also says he's a veteran, though he doesn't say what branch of service, and the military says it has no record of him. Last night, Barbara Clark took a camera crew to his house to see if we could finally get a statement. Like every other attempt, it proved futile. We were, however, able to talk briefly with a neighbor.

(*Lights down on BRANSON.*)

(*Lights up on BARBARA CLARK, standing in darkness. The sound of crickets.*)

BARBARA CLARK: I'm standing outside John Smith's home, and, though we believe he's inside, no one has come to the door. But we have been speaking with his neighbor, Leo Dorn. Mr. Dorn, your thoughts on John Smith?

LEO DORN: He's an all right guy. Don't see him much. Has a dog. Rides a bicycle.

BARBARA CLARK: Are you going to vote for him?

LEO DORN: For what?

BARBARA CLARK: For mayor. In tomorrow's election.

LEO DORN: That tomorrow?

BARBARA CLARK: Yes. Are you going to vote for Smith, or for his opponent, Shawn Tigon?

LEO DORN: Oh, I haven't voted in years. Every election's the same, far as I'm concerned.

BARBARA CLARK: Shawn Tigon has promised to change that.

LEO DORN: Tigon? Who's he?

BARBARA CLARK: (*To camera.*) Lloyd, back to you.

(*Lights down on BARBARA CLARK.*)

(*Lights up on LLOYD BRANSON.*)

LLOYD BRANSON: That was Smith's last chance to talk to the media before the people of Home Haven went to the polls. They're voting right now, and I'm here to take an informal exit poll.

(*VOTER #1 enters.*)

LLOYD BRANSON: Excuse me. Can I ask who you voted for?

VOTER #1: Smith.

LLOYD BRANSON: Would you mind telling me why?

VOTER #1: I believe he's the right man for the job.

LLOYD BRANSON: Why is that?

VOTER #1: I have no idea. I don't like to overthink things. Thinking too much only leads to problems.

LLOYD BRANSON: What kind of problems?

VOTER #1: Never thought about it.

(*VOTER #1 exits.*)

(*VOTER #2 enters.*)

LLOYD BRANSON: Excuse me. Would you mind telling us who you voted for?

VOTER #2: Smith. I like his name. It's a good, strong name.

LLOYD BRANSON: What about his opponent's name?

VOTER #2: Shawn Tigon . . . What kind of name is that? It's . . . different.

(*VOTER #2 exits.*)

(*VOTER #3 enters.*)

LLOYD BRANSON: Who did you vote for?

VOTER #3: Smith. He was born here. He's one of us.

LLOYD BRANSON: Shawn Tigon was born here, too.

VOTER #3: He was? I didn't know that.

(VOTER #3 exits.)

(VOTER #4 enters.)

LLOYD BRANSON: Would you mind telling us who you voted for?

VOTER #4: Smith.

LLOYD BRANSON: Why not Tigon?

VOTER #4: He's not one of us. He's . . . different.

LLOYD BRANSON: In what way?

VOTER #4: It's hard to say. It's just something you feel in your gut. And once that feeling is there, it's just there, you know what I mean?

LLOYD BRANSON: So Tigon is "different," but you can't say why.

VOTER #4: See? You feel it too. You know what I'm talking about. You know what I mean. Know what I mean?

(VOTER #4 exits.)

(VOTER #5 enters.)

LLOYD BRANSON: Excuse me . . . Who did you vote for?

VOTER #5: Smith. He's got experience.

LLOYD BRANSON: But he's never been elected to office. Shawn Tigon has served on two city commissions.

VOTER #5: Tigon's a paramedic. Smith's a politician. He said so, on his petition.

(VOTER #5 exits.)

(VOTER #6 enters.)

LLOYD BRANSON: Excuse me. Would you tell us who you voted for?

VOTER #6: Smith. He's a guy you can have a beer with.

LLOYD BRANSON: What about Tigon?

VOTER #6: He doesn't drink beer. I saw him say that in that TV interview.

LLOYD BRANSON: The next day he said that was a joke.

VOTER #6: Well, maybe there are some things you shouldn't joke about.

LLOYD BRANSON: Does Smith like beer?

VOTER #6: How do I know? Geez, it's only an expression!

(VOTER #6 exits.)

(VOTER #7 enters.)

LLOYD BRANSON: Who did you vote for?

VOTER #7: I voted for Smith. He doesn't make those long speeches, the way the others do, just going on and on and on and on and on and on. Says what he has to, and then has the sense to keep quiet and let that be enough. Doesn't go into all those long, unnecessary details. Doesn't let things get all cluttered up with things he doesn't have to say. And best of all, he doesn't keep repeating himself. Lets his words speak for themselves.

LLOYD BRANSON: He hasn't made a single statement during the whole campaign.

VOTER #7: Well, there ya go.

LLOYD BRANSON: What about his record?

VOTER #7: That speaks for itself, too.

LLOYD BRANSON: He has no record.

VOTER #7: See? He's honest. Has no record. Never committed a crime. Or never been caught. And that shows he's smart!

(VOTER #7 exits.)

(VOTER #8 enters.)

LLOYD BRANSON: Would you mind telling us who you voted for?

VOTER #8: Smith. He's strong. Decisive. You see how he handled the press during the campaign?

LLOYD BRANSON: He refused to talk to the press.

VOTER #8: Right! Stood up to them like a solid wall! Wouldn't give in, no matter what! Knew he was right and stuck to his guns! That's the kind of guy we need!

(VOTER #8 exits.)

(VOTER #9 enters.)

LLOYD BRANSON: Who did you vote for today?

VOTER #9: I voted for Smith. The other guy is too wishy-washy. He changed his stand too many times during the campaign.

LLOYD BRANSON: Tigon changed his mind on one issue. He supported a bill because he thought it would bring jobs to town, then changed his mind when he saw it would cost jobs.

VOTER #9: See what I mean? Wishy-washy.

LLOYD BRANSON: Doesn't that show he thinks about things? That he's willing to reconsider a position and change his mind if he feels he's made a mistake?

VOTER #9: Yeah. And that's exactly what I'm talkin' about.

(VOTER #9 exits.)

(VOTER #10 enters.)

LLOYD BRANSON: Excuse me. We're taking an informal exit poll. Who did you vote for?

VOTER #10: Smith! He's a veteran. The man loves his country!

LLOYD BRANSON: He says he's a veteran, but there are no records to back that up.

VOTER #10: Well, those things happen. But he served. That's what counts. He's a brave, patriotic, loyal American. What's the other guy done for his country?

LLOYD BRANSON: Tigon is a paramedic who often works seven days a week and does double shifts. And he was a rescue worker after 9/11.

VOTER #10: He was? I didn't know that.

LLOYD BRANSON: Does that make you wish you voted for him instead?

VOTER #10: Nah. Made up my mind on day one. You know how these guys are. All say the same thing. Which is anything they think'll get 'em elected. They must think we're all a bunch of dummies.

(*VOTER #10 exits.*)

(*VOTER # 11 enters.*)

LLOYD BRANSON: Excuse me. Who did you vote for?

VOTER #11: Shawn Tigon.

LLOYD BRANSON: Why?

VOTER # 11: I like his name! Reminds me of . . . the smell of a new car.

(*VOTER #11 exits.*)

(*VOTER # 12 enters.*)

LLOYD BRANSON: And who did you vote for?

VOTER #12: Oh, I voted for Tigon. He's wants to lower city sales taxes.

LLOYD BRANSON: He said he was in favor of a slightly higher city sales tax if the money was used for more police, fire protection, and teachers.

VOTER #12: Well, I'm for fewer taxes, not more!

(*VOTER # 12 exits.*)

LLOYD BRANSON: (*To camera.*) I'm getting word that we'll probably soon be able to declare a winner. Nevertheless, I'll remain here, talking with voters, as we attempt to answer the question, "What are these people thinking?" Hold on . . . I've just been told that, with most of the vote now in, we are able to declare a winner in Home Haven's race for mayor. That winner is John Smith. I'm also being told that Mayor-elect Smith has finally agreed to talk to us, but only by phone. We go now to Barbara Clark, on the phone with Home Haven's new mayor.

(*Lights down on BRANSON.*)

(*Lights up half, on bare stage.*)

BARBARA CLARK: (*On phone.*) Lloyd, I have Mayor-elect John Smith on the phone. He's agreed to make a statement, but will not take any questions. Mr. Smith, ready when you are.

JOHN SMITH: (*On phone.*) This is a great day for democracy. The people have spoken, and I promise you this: You are going to get the government you deserve.

(He hangs up. The sound of a dial tone . . . This goes on for several seconds, as)

(Slow fade to black.)

WAITING FOR THE LEFTY

by Tira Palmquist

Original production by
Mile Square Theatre
Hoboken, NJ
Producer: Chris O'Connor, Artistic Director

Produced at the 14th Annual 7th *Inning Stretch:* Seven Ten-Minute Plays
About Baseball
May 18–20, 2018

Director, Jack Cummins

JOHNSON, Taylor Graves
RIVERA, Andrew Baldwin (* *in this production,* RIVERA*'s name was*
    changed to PLANK)
WAGNER, Adam Maggio

Set: Matt Fick
Sound: Matt Fick
Projections: Elise Irabarne
Lighting: Justin McCormick
Costumes: Jack Cummins
Stage Manager: Erin Collins

CHARACTERS

WAGNER, M. 30s. A long reliever. A hot head. A man truly dissatisfied with his current lot in life.

RIVERA, M. Early 20s. Middle reliever. This is his first minor league contract, and could not be more pleased. The most positive man in baseball. Endlessly happy.

JOHNSON, W. 20s. The Lefty. She might be the best pitcher of her generation, but is, you know, a woman.

SETTING

The home ballpark of a minor league team.

TIME

Now.

NOTE

The play includes several shifts in time. Keep it simple—lights and sound shifting to indicate the jumps in time—without indulging in blackouts.

PREGAME

The murmur of a stadium crowd. The bullpen of a minor league baseball team. Two relief pitchers are standing and watching warmups, or something. One of them has a bag of sunflower seeds. If there's a fence, they lean on it. They may have been watching for awhile. They are good at watching. It's what they do.

WAGNER: Do you ever think that things have gotta change?

RIVERA: Nope.

WAGNER: Not ever? Not once?

RIVERA: Nah. Things are great! The weather is beautiful! It's a great day for baseball!

WAGNER: The baseball we never get to play?

RIVERA: What are you talking about?

WAGNER: (*Gesturing out at the field.*) I'm talking about Mitchell. I'm talking about Janorek. When was the last time you got to pitch. I'm telling you—we are gettin' no opportunities. We deserve opportunities.

RIVERA: Everything's great. Our day will come. Don't rock the boat.

WAGNER: Plus we're gonna be saddled with the new lefty.

RIVERA: Right! Johnson! I wonder when Johnson's showing up.

WAGNER: Today. We didn't need a new lefty. We had a great lefty.

RIVERA: You mean the great lefty who's out on waivers?

WAGNER: I liked Wilson.

RIVERA: Yeah, well, Wilson's gone. And we need a lefty.

(Looking around.)

Is there something different around here?

(A new pitcher arrives. And it's clearly a woman.)

JOHNSON: Hey. How you doing?

(WAGNER stares, dumbfounded. The crack of a bat. The crowd roars. The organ plays.)

FIRST INNING

From a speaker somewhere: "PLAY BALL" The crowd roars. WAGNER is standing near the new pitcher, who's sitting, feet up on a bucket, totally unconcerned with his attention.

WAGNER: You can't be in here.

RIVERA: I know what's different! The bench! We used to have a bench!

WAGNER: Hey: You. You can't be in here.

(She looks up at him. To JOHNSON.)

Girlfriends can't hang out in the bullpen.

JOHNSON: . . . yeah?

WAGNER: So—you know . . .

JOHNSON: If I see my girlfriend, I'll tell her.

(She lowers her cap over her eyes, as if to take a nap.)

RIVERA: Where the hell is the bench?

WAGNER: Would you shut up about the bench?

RIVERA: But we used to have a bench. It was a real nice bench. Now we have folding chairs?

JOHNSON: Repossessed?

(RIVERA finally looks at her. She raises her cap.)

RIVERA: What?

JOHNSON: Maybe that's what happened. That's what happens when you don't pay your bills.

RIVERA: They can repossess a bench? Why would they repossess a bench?

WAGNER: We're not talking about the bench anymore!

JOHNSON: Maybe you're not talking about the bench. But we are. (*To Rivera.*) *Johnson.*

RIVERA: Hey, Johnson. Rivera.

(They shake hands.)

WAGNER: Don't shake her hand! You can't shake her hand!

(RIVERA is completely flummoxed. JOHNSON tries to get comfortable on the folding chair and bucket situation.)

JOHNSON: (*To RIVERA.*) You're right. You need a bench.

WAGNER: Who the hell are you?

JOHNSON: Oh. Sorry. Didn't I say? I'm your new lefty. Lou Johnson.

(The crack of a bat. The crowd roars. The organ plays.)

THIRD INNING

(JOHNSON now has the bag of sunflower seeds, flanked by the other pitchers. RIVERA is sitting next to her, just chatting. WAGNER, on the

other hand, appears to be in a serious negotiation.)

WAGNER: Yeah—but you're not listening.

JOHNSON: (*To RIVERA.*) You're telling me: Mitchell never burns? He always pitches?

RIVERA: Always. Well, there was that week he had his tonsils out.

WAGNER: You can't be our lefty—

JOHNSON: (*To WAGNER.*) Uh, yeah I can. (*To RIVERA.*) So how many games'd he miss—for the tonsils?

RIVERA: None—he was out for just the first couple innings. Janorek's our second, and he started us out—and Wagner—he's a long reliever—he was PISSED, let me tell you. He thought he'd be pitching, for sure.

JOHNSON: Mitchell came back? That same day?

WAGNER: But you're—

RIVERA: Yep. He's a tank. A monster. A machine.

JOHNSON: What about you?

RIVERA: Me? I'm middle relief. Number five.

JOHNSON: Ooooh. Fuck.

RIVERA: Nah, nah. It's fine. I just gotta be patient.

WAGNER: WOULD YOU TWO STOP IT.

JOHNSON: What?

RIVERA: What?

WAGNER: YOU'RE A WOMAN.

JOHNSON: I know!

RIVERA: We know!

WAGNER: So . . . you can't be here!

JOHNSON: And yet I am.

(Holding out the bag to him.)

Seeds?

(The crack of a bat. The crowd roars. The organ plays.)

FIFTH INNING

(JOHNSON appears to be warming up. Not pitching—just stretching. Just getting warm. WAGNER has pulled RIVERA away from JOHNSON. Another negotiation.)

RIVERA: I don't see what your problem is.

WAGNER: My problem is that our lefty is a woman—

JOHNSON: Who can hear you.

WAGNER: *(Tries to shuffle further away from her.)* We already don't get enough pitching time. And now this?

RIVERA: You got a problem with her because she's a woman?

WAGNER: Yes because she's a woman!

JOHNSON: Who is still standing right here!

WAGNER: *(To JOHNSON.)* OK. Look, no disrespect, but—

JOHNSON: You know when someone says that, it's gonna be totally disrespectful, right?

WAGNER: Women can't pitch.

JOHNSON: Oooooookay—

RIVERA: Ohhhh duuuuuuude—

JOHNSON: One, Women in fact do pitch, so when you say "can't," I think you mean, "shouldn't."

WAGNER: OK. Maybe you can in, like, softball, which is totally great, but I'm talking about overhand pitching, which requires a completely different physiology.

JOHNSON: The last time I checked, there was remarkably little anatomical difference between male and female deltoids—

RIVERA: Yeah—that was seriously uncool, Wagner.

JOHNSON: And coach says he needs me warmed up, so—

(She returns to warming up. WAGNER pulls RIVERA further away.)

RIVERA: What is with you, dude?

WAGNER: Oh, Rivera: lemme tell you: We're gonna strike.

(The crack of a bat. The crowd roars. The organ plays.)

SEVENTH INNING

(JOHNSON is now warming up and pitching—either to an unseen individual, or to RIVERA—and WAGNER is practically incandescent with rage.)

WAGNER: Rivera! What are you doing?

RIVERA: . . . helping?

WAGNER: Well, stop it! Don't help her! She's the enemy!

JOHNSON: I'm not the enemy.

RIVERA: She's not the enemy. You know who the enemy is? Management. That's who the enemy is.

JOHNSON: I don't know why you're so keyed up, anyway. I'm just another pitcher. You were expecting another pitcher, right?

WAGNER: (*Scoffing.*) You're just another pitcher.

JOHNSON: That's right.

WAGNER: OK, then, Just Another Pitcher—what are your pitches?

JOHNSON: You're gonna quiz me about my pitches?

WAGNER: That's right.

RIVERA: So far, she's pitched a fastball, a curve—

WAGNER: Rivera—

RIVERA: A slider, a great changeup—

JOHNSON: Hey. Thanks.

RIVERA: A split finger fastball—

WAGNER: Shut it! Both of you! (*To RIVERA.*) That's it. You and me: we're going on strike.

JOHNSON: What are you talking about?

WAGNER: You stay out of this. (*To RIVERA.*) Come on: a walkout. A planned protest. A "workers controlling the means of production" thing.

RIVERA: Uh . . . I didn't know you were a commie.

WAGNER: I'm not a commie! But we'll show them what happens when we refuse to pitch!

RIVERA: I never pitch already!

JOHNSON: No, it makes sense to me.

WAGNER: I'm not asking you.

JOHNSON: OK, but I'm saying. You want them to get 'em to notice you? You gotta make some noise. (*Beat.*) Look. Coach is signaling. I gotta go. Thanks for the help.

   (*Shakes Rivera's hand.*)

RIVERA: How's the arm?

JOHNSON: Great. Thanks.

RIVERA: Show 'em who's boss!

   (*She jogs off.*)

WAGNER: What is wrong with you?

RIVERA: Nothing! She's nice!

WAGNER: She's nice? You're crazy!

   (*We hear the crowd cheering.*)

You and me: we're dying by inches here. Every game. Here, on the bench.

RIVERA: They took our bench.

WAGNER: And they took our bench! It's a slow death or fight! It's a war, I tell you!

RIVERA: Are we still talking about baseball?

(We hear the ump's cry: Strike! The crowd goes cheers. RIVERA is now watching JOHNSON pitch.)

RIVERA: Shit—look at her. She's fearless.

WAGNER: No: it's you and me: we unite, and fight! And we strike!

(Again, the ump's cry: STRIKE! RIVERA cheers at this.)

RIVERA: My god! Look at her! Strike!

WAGNER: That's right: Strike! Louder! Come on: Strike. Strike. Strike. Strike.

(He removes his jersey to wave it over his head, like a flag, while RIVERA is clapping and cheering JOHNSON.)

RIVERA: Come on, Johnson! Strike! Strike!

WAGNER: Strike—Strike—Strike!

(And the ump's final call: STRIKE! The crowd goes mad. The men continue shouting—and then, WAGNER realizes why RIVERA is shouting, crumples to his knees, as RIVERA, and the crowd, keep cheering.)

(Lights fade as the cheering increases.)

WE THE SISTERS

by Laura Neill

First produced by
Fresh Ink Theatre
Boston Theatre Marathon
May 6, 2018

Director, Claire Whitehouse

LARA, Louise Hamill
BECKY, Victoria George

CHARACTERS

LARA SWEET, 30s, a conservative Congresswoman. Ivy League educated.
   Plans on running for President in the next twenty years.
BECKY SILVER, 30s, a yoga teacher. Ivy League educated. Plans from
   paycheck to paycheck.

TIME

The day before the next healthcare repeal bill goes to a vote.

SETTING

The office of Congresswoman Lara Sweet. Washington, D.C.

A NOTE ON PUNCTUATION

A slash / indicates an overlap. The next line begins at the / .

A small but sophisticated office. Congresswoman LARA SWEET sits behind her desk, a large American flag taking up most of the space behind her. The door swings open. BECKY SILVER enters, singing a sorority chant loudly at LARA.

BECKY: HOTTEST SMARTEST STATE OF ART-EST
WHO IS THAT YOU SEE?
YOU'RE THE REST
WE'RE THE BEST

BECKY and LARA: WE'RE THE EZT!
SOOOOO . . . DRINK!

> *(LARA jumps up from her desk, laughing, and comes to embrace BECKY.)*

LARA: Becky Silver, oh my God!

BECKY: You still don't know how to sing.

LARA: And you still hug like a gorilla.

BECKY: I'm usually a lot drunker when I sing that song.

LARA: Well, if you'd like to increase your BAC . . .

> *(She gestures to her office bar.)*

BECKY: Always.

> *(LARA pours drinks as BECKY makes herself at home.)*

LARA: You're in town for the week? I have to say, when my assistant / told me

BECKY: (*Re: "assistant".*) / Look at you, girl.

LARA: / that Becky Silver was in my office—Jesus, woman. You in town for a bachelorette? Work trip? You're a yoga coach now, right, in / California?

BECKY: / Teacher, or guide, Congresswoman, people don't really coach yoga.

LARA: Well, excuuuuuse / me.

BECKY: / But I quit to take care of my mom.

LARA: Oh. I'm so sorry, I didn't know.

BECKY: It's okay, I didn't expect you to.

LARA: So you're out here for good now?

BECKY: Ain't nobody else to take care of her. SOOOOO . . . DRINK!

(She chugs the drink LARA gave her. LARA tries to change the subject.)

LARA: . . . So are you . . . married? Boyfriend? Girlfriend? You always had a great set of, what were they called, embarrassing stories, we had a word for embarrassing—

BECKY: Ediths!

LARA: Ediths! Any Ediths to share? I have to toe the line these days and need to live vicariously . . .

BECKY: Oh yeah, I broke into a building the other day, had sex on the roof and then jumped off the fire escape with a coupla cops chasing me.

LARA: You're kidding.

BECKY: Yeah. Full-time caretaking kinda makes it hard to get out on the town.

LARA: But you've gotta take a day off sometimes. The great / Becky Silver—

BECKY: Lara, I need you to vote no tomorrow.

(Pause.)

LARA: Is it time for the alum election?

BECKY: You know what I mean.

LARA: No, Becky, I don't. You must be referring to some backwater alumnae election for EZT secretary or some shit like that, because there is no possible way—

BECKY: I'm talking about Scalise-Abraham, Congresswoman. The repeal. The thirty-six-hundredth Obamacare repeal your party is trying to push through Congress.

LARA: "Old times' sake," fuck you. Bobby said you wanted a quick drink—

BECKY: I came here to tell you—

LARA: Nobody tells me how to vote, Becky.

BECKY: Except Paul Ryan.

LARA: Nobody.

BECKY: My mother has a preexisting condition, Lara.

LARA: This little chat is over.

(Over the next few lines, LARA rises and casually makes her way over to the panic button under her desk.)

BECKY: You don't even know what I mean by that, you don't even know what she has, because not only did you de-friend me on Facebook the second you ran for City Council, the list of goddamn preexisting conditions that insurance doesn't have to cover anymore is TWO HUNDRED PAGES LONG, it's TWO HUNDRED FUCKING PAGES—

LARA: Don't make me throw you out, Becky. I'd really rather not do that—

BECKY: You're not going to do that, Lara.

LARA: No, because for old times' sake—

BECKY: BullSHIT.

LARA: For old times' sake I'm going to let you calmly collect yourself and then walk out into that hallway without Bobby's foot up your buttcrack because you are better than this. You should be so much better than this.

BECKY: EN 706.

(Pause.)

LARA: You think a random collection of letters and numbers is going to help you?

BECKY: Plagiarism. Academic dishonesty. Let's call it what it is, cheating—

LARA: I don't know what you're talking about.

BECKY: I think you do know, Congresswoman. I think you remember very clearly how I helped you copy-and-paste your final paper for your senior

English seminar. I think you remember very, very clearly how you were in tears because your thesis advisor had told you that you were getting a B and losing Phi Beta Kappa and how you were in the 1902 room shoveling peanut butter cookies into your face moaning that your life was fucking over and how could you go on and how you begged me, begged me, ON YOUR KNEES BEGGED ME to bring you a fucking Four Loko and some weed because you wanted to get real high and forget all your problems. And I think you remember how instead of getting you wasted, I sat you down and googled with you until we found a nice-looking old dissertation from the University of Michigan. And I'm very, very sure you remember sending that in to your professor and holding your breath for the next fourteen days praying that no one would put it through Turn It In, and getting real drunk with me graduation morning when you realized they hadn't. When you realized you had graduated Dartmouth College on a lie . . . I'm absolutely certain you remember all that. Because you might have your hand on that panic button but you haven't pressed it yet.

(Pause. Then LARA bursts out laughing.)

LARA: Jesus, Becky, you had me going there for a minute. Tryna act like this is Watergate or some shit. Girl, chill out and drink your drink.

BECKY: Oh, now we're friends.

LARA: You're hilarious. Bringing up that old shit—

BECKY: Acting like some college slang and some "drank" is gonna keep me from squealing.

LARA: Becky. You're not going to "squeal" anything.

BECKY: Am I not?

LARA: Some age-old college thing isn't going to hurt me at all, Becky, you know that. And I don't think you want to get famous as that bitter old frenemy who realized that even with her Ivy League degree she STILL ended up as an aging yoga coach because she couldn't take the pressure of Harvard Law, you don't want to be that bitter ugly woman on CNN. Not when your momma's watching.

BECKY: Do you know how much levodopa / costs?

LARA: / Would your mother be proud of you for bursting into my / office?

BECKY: / Do you know how low my mother's pain tolerance / is?

LARA: / She doesn't want her daughter / to be a blackmailer.

BECKY: / You think she wants to pay thirty-six THOUSAND dollars a month to be able to feel like herself? Talk like herself? To LIVE?

(He voice breaks as she shouts. LARA pauses.)

LARA: I think Scalise-Abraham is a fair, comprehensive healthcare bill that will restore justice to millions of middle-class Americans.

BECKY: You better just press the damn panic button already. Because I'm not leaving until you vote no.

LARA: Like I'm going to let a yoga coach determine my vote in the United States / Congress—

BECKY: / Will you stop saying yoga coach. I am glad I dropped out of law school—

LARA: You can't blackmail me.

BECKY: Oh, but I can. That Ivy League degree comes off that wall? Bet that nice little name plaque comes off that desk. It'd be one hell of an Edith, wouldn't it?

LARA: Becky.

(She regroups.)

 . . . were we ever sisters?

BECKY: What?

LARA: You took the pledge the same as I did. You come in here with our fight song, drink with me, remind me of that time you did something really, really beautiful for me, that time you saved me from myself. I could've jumped in the fucking river that night, I really could've. And you saved me. You and your Smirnoff-icing, fire-alarm-setting-off, stank-ass self, you SAVED me. Because we were sisters. We were Thetas. We ARE SISTERS.

BECKY: If we were sisters, you'd care about my mom.

LARA: I do care about your mom, Becky. And I'm perfectly willing to help you out, personally. As a friend, as your sister, as someone who is genuinely grateful for all of your love and support and friendship over the years, I'm willing to help you out.

BECKY: By voting no.

LARA: By helping with your mom's expenses.

BECKY: . . . Congresswoman.

LARA: You did something really nice for me that night, Becky. I'd like to do something really nice for you.

BECKY: How nice?

LARA: Really nice.

BECKY: HOW MANY SUBCUTANEOUS WAKING DAY APOMORPHINE INFUSIONS NICE?

LARA: As many as your mother needs. As many as you need. Hey.

(She reaches out to hold BECKY's hand.)

We're sisters, you and me. I'm here for you.

(BECKY stares at LARA's hand.)

BECKY: What about everyone else's mother?

LARA: Your mother should be most important to you.

BECKY: What about everyone else who doesn't have a sorority sister who's, who's—

LARA: THIS IS NOT ABOUT EVERYONE ELSE. THIS IS ABOUT YOUR MOTHER.

(Pause.)

BECKY: . . . Thank you.

(LARA gets her checkbook and starts to write a check.)

Thank you for reminding me what my mother would want me to do.

(She takes her drink and throws it in LARA's face. LARA does not recoil. Instead, she snaps.)

LARA: You fucking idiot. If you can't see that this is your mother's only chance—you fucking child. We're not in college anymore, Becky; we're not in the land of throwing drinks on each other when we disagree. We are not in the land of Keystone Light and senior year and setting off the fire alarm at three in the morning with our fucking popcorn and *Buffy the Vampire Slayer*, we are not the EZT. We are adults now. And look at the kind of adults we are. You are a yoga coach who can't make enough money to buy her mother's medicine. I am the future first female president of the United States of America.

You are the rest and I am the best. And when I offer you something you take it.

   (BECKY starts to exit.)

Oh, grow up, Becky. You're gonna let your little games cause your mother pain? Because if you don't take this check, that's what you're doing. You can throw sixty-dollar scotch in my face and storm out my office all you want, but her pain tolerance is just gonna get lower . . . and lower . . . and lower . . . and Scalise-Abraham is gonna pass. If not tomorrow, then soon. And your mother is in pain. You've spent your entire life being a terrible fucking disappointment, saddling your mother with your college debt, dropping out of law school, shattering all the hopes she had for you one by one . . . Are you really going to disappoint her again? You better think really hard before you walk out that door. Because if you're going to be a child, you sure as hell better be a good one.

   (She finishes the check and holds it out. BECKY stares at the check.)

BECKY: She has Parkinson's, Lara. She is in a lot of pain . . . You have no idea how much.

   (Then she takes the check. Holding LARA's check, she leaves the office.)

WILD BIRDS

by Nicole Pandolfo

Original production by
Hudson Theatre Works
May 11, 2018
Weehawken, New Jersey

Director, Tara Cioletti

LANA, Molly Collier
NEO, Kevin Cristaldi

CHARACTERS

NEO, 20s–30s.
LANA, 20s–30s.

SETTING

A bird store.

TIME

Present day.

Lights up on LANA, behind the counter of Birds Birds Birds Nature and Retail Supply Store. There is the ambient noise of birds chirping and feathers ruffling. LANA is playing a game on her cellphone which makes various ding and zoink noises. The bell of the entrance door rings and NEO enters carrying a cage with a scarf draped over it, obscuring the contents. LANA bounces out of her seat.

LANA: Welcome to *Birds Birds Birds Nature and Retail*. How can I help you?

NEO: Uh. Hi.

LANA: Hi. How can I help you?

NEO: Is Jeb here?

LANA: Jeb the owner?

NEO: Yeah. Is he here?

LANA: No.

NEO: How about the manager?

LANA: Jeb is the manager.

NEO: Well, do you know when he'll be back?

LANA: Six to eight weeks. He's in rehab in Jacksonville.

NEO: Oh . . .

(He turns to leave.)

LANA: Is there something I can help you with?

NEO: It's really the kind of thing I should speak with Jeb about.

LANA: Jeb put me in charge until he gets back. (*Beat.*) It's my chance to make a good impression. Maybe even get a raise out of it. I'm the one who convinced him to get into NA you know.

NEO: Oh. Congrats.

LANA: Thanks. So tell me, what can I help you with?

NEO: I . . . um . . . have a bird you may be interested in purchasing.

LANA: Well we aren't really in the buying birds business. We're in the selling birds business.

NEO: I think you're gonna wanna buy this one.

(He puts the cage on the counter. LANA pulls up the scarf and takes a look. She freezes.)

LANA: Oh my God.

NEO: I told you.

LANA: That's a Kakapo.

NEO: I know.

LANA: I've never seen a Kakapo live and in the flesh. I've dreamt about it, but never ever thought it would happen.

NEO: Her name's Deena.

LANA: Deena. She's stunning.

NEO: Thank you.

LANA: Kakapos are one of the most rare birds on the planet. Known as the night parrot, they're a native of New Zealand and the only kind of parrot that can't fly. Fortunately for them they can climb like a mo-fo . . . They're also on the endangered species list, which means not only is there no monetary value one can even place upon them, but that buying and selling one is surely illegal.

NEO: Wow. You know your birds.

LANA: Yeah.

NEO: That's why I wanted to talk to the owner. I know from a friend of a friend that he is willing to deal in rare birds.

LANA: Rare is different than on the verge of extinction. *(Beat.)* Where's her radio transmitter?

NEO: Clipped before she was transported. Naturally.

LANA: How did you get her here from New Zealand without anyone noticing?

NEO: I can't tell you that.

LANA: If you don't tell me then this conversation is over.

(*A beat.*)

NEO: That information could put your life in danger.

LANA: . . . Doubtful.

(*A beat.*)

NEO: I know a guy who knows a guy who knows a guy who works at the Kakapo conservation. Deena was smuggled here through a series of trips in the cargo hold of various mid-level cruise ships.

(*A beat.*)

LANA: An endangered species black market . . . Is nothing sacred anymore?

(*A beat. NEO starts to go.*)

NEO: Look, if you're not interested/

LANA: Wait. She is beautiful. And if I don't take her, she could end up in the hands of some ill-intentioned birder who won't love her nearly as much as I will . . . What price did you have in mind?

(*A beat.*)

NEO: One hundred thousand dollars.

LANA: A hundred thousand?!

NEO: Yeah.

LANA: That's insane.

NEO: That's the price.

LANA: We're *Birds Birds Birds* not the Federal Reserve. Who has that kind of cash lying around?

NEO: I heard that would not be an unreasonable sum for a man like Jeb. He is after all a descendant of oil barons.

LANA: Where'd you hear that?

NEO: Wikipedia.

(*Beat.*)

He has a trust fund.

LANA: Jeb might, but *Birds Birds Birds* doesn't have a hundred thousand just lying around. You think we just keep that kind of cash in a safe in the back next to the bird-washing basin by the mini fridge?

NEO: I guess I'll just have to take my business elsewhere then.

    (He turns to go.)

LANA: Jesus you play hard to get. *(Beat.)* A hundred thousand?

NEO: A hundred thousand.

LANA: That's a lot of money.

NEO: Deena's a lot of bird.

LANA: What do you need that kind of cash for?

NEO: That's none of your business.

LANA: It is my business if you want me to buy your bird from you. I'm sure that would be preferable to schlepping around to other, inferior bird stores. Wouldn't want word to get around that you're trying to sell an endangered species would you? I feel like that's the kind of thing the FBI is not a huge fan of.

    (Beat.)

NEO: I need the cash so I can buy supplies.

LANA: Supplies for what?

    (A beat.)

NEO: World devastation.

LANA: Huh?

NEO: We've got various wing nuts running the world each trying to prove their scrotum sacs are bigger than the others' and I'm being realistic and want to hedge my bets. Could be Russia, could be North Korea, hey, could even be Pakistan, but trust me, someone is going to drop that bomb and thanks to Deena here, when they do, I'm gonna be ready to pick up the shards of humanity. It's my destiny.

LANA: Um. Isn't that a little far-fetched?

NEO: Far-fetched? Was *1984* far-fetched? How about *The Manchurian Candidate*?

LANA: How about *The Matrix*?

NEO: Exactly. As a person willing to look adversity in the face I feel it is my duty to humanity to be prepared.

LANA: What the heck do you need to buy that costs a hundred thousand dollars?

NEO: Hundred thousand? Please. I could use a million, but we start where we can start.
    I need a hazmat suit, a hazmat suit for a guest, a sniper rifle and multiple rounds of ammunition. Grenades. A year's supply of enough antibiotics to cure a small elementary school of common bacterial ailments. Dried food. Jugs of water and several portable water filters. Batteries. A crank-radio. A suturing kit. Board games, and if I'm lucky, a bazooka.

LANA: A bazooka? Really?

NEO: I know a guy who knows a guy who has one in his basement.

LANA: Doesn't the military have all that stuff?

NEO: You're assuming the ones attacking us aren't them.

LANA: And you feel it's your responsibility to society to begin preparing for a nuclear Armageddon that will either be perpetrated against us by one of the world's megalomaniacal dictators or possibly by our own US military?

NEO: Exactly.

    (Beat.)

LANA: Welp, I still think it's a tad fantastical, but you know what, I'm one of those people who never thought in a zillion years Donald Trump would be our president and so to that I say, I guess you never know.

NEO: You never know.

LANA: Ok, wait here.

(She exits to the back. NEO composes himself, then takes a look under the scarf at Deena.)

(LANA reenters, carrying an envelope. NEO straightens himself.)

LANA: I can offer you forty thousand.

NEO: Forty? No way.

(He grabs the cage to exit.)

LANA: Ok fine. Fifty thousand and I don't call the police and tell them what you're trying to sell. (*A beat.*) It's my best offer.

(She puts the envelope on the counter.)

NEO: I'll have to take the bazooka off my wish list.

(LANA shrugs. A beat. She extends her hand to shake. A moment goes by and NEO extends his hand to her as well. NEO puts Deena on the counter and pushes the cage towards Lana. He takes the envelope and looks inside, then back at LANA.)

LANA: Pleasure doing business with you . . . actually, I don't think I caught your name.

(NEO turns to go.)

NEO: Call me Neo.

(He exits and LANA watches him leave. After a beat she lifts the scarf off Deena's cage.)

(Lights hard to black.)

YOU WERE AWESOME!

by Bob Zaslow

Production by
Tompkins Corners Cultural Center
Putnam Valley, New York
August 31 and September 1, 2018

Codirected by Paul and Judy Allen

Actors: Paul Savior and Judy Allen

CHARACTERS

STEVEN, a still dashing, sixty-something former soap opera star who
    drinks too much and listens too little.
RUTHIE, a pharmaceutical salesperson in her fifties, who's learned to dance
    like there's no one watching.

*STEVEN's apartment on the upper west side, around ten o'clock in the morning
and after a massive party. The place is a mess. He wakes and rises slowly from
his sofa, opening his eyes to a strangely upbeat woman who has been happily
tidying up.*

STEVEN: Who are you?

RUTHIE: Good morning, Steven!

STEVEN: Who are you?

RUTHIE: You're so funny.

STEVEN: Where's Leesa?

RUTHIE: Which one was Leesa?

STEVEN: My girlfriend . . . fiancé. Platinum blonde hair. Glasses.

RUTHIE: Oh. She left early. She said something about how she really never knew you before.

STEVEN: Leesa said that? You're sure that was Leesa?

RUTHIE: (*Holding up engagement ring.*) She threw this in the garbage.

STEVEN: (*Totally waking up.*) Oh, my God! Our ring! What did I do?

RUTHIE: Oh, you were awesome! She can't take a joke, that's all.

STEVEN: What was I joking about?

RUTHIE: Oh, come on! You don't remember?

STEVEN: Please . . . uh . . .

RUTHIE: Ruthie . . .

STEVEN: Ruthie . . . what did I do at the party?

RUTHIE: You honestly don't remember?

STEVEN: (*Losing patience.*) What. Did. I. Do!?

RUTHIE: Well first, you made a toast to all the women in the room and offered a twenty-dollar bill to any girl who was wearing a pink bra to take it off.

STEVEN: Oh no . . .

RUTHIE: (*Holding up pink bra.*) Yes.

STEVEN: Is that it? What did she do?

RUTHIE: No. That wasn't the awesomest part. Then you offered another twenty to any girl who was wearing pink panties.

STEVEN: Don't tell me.

RUTHIE: (*She holds up pink panties.*) Ta da!

STEVEN: And that's when she left? Did she slap me?

RUTHIE: No. I have to tell you, I didn't know she was your girlfriend until later. But she didn't leave then either . . .

STEVEN: OK, OK . . . what a jerk.

RUTHIE: No, you were awesome! Although I don't think that guy you called your " little bro" was too thrilled when you announced to the entire room that he wet his bed until he was nine years old.

STEVEN: No. No. No. Marty!

RUTHIE: He was laughing at first. Really. But that's why . . .

STEVEN: That's why what? What happened?

RUTHIE: That's why there's a big wine stain on your carpet. I tried to get it out with club soda, but I guess it was one of those sweet red ones . . . like a Merlot or something. I got most of the wine out of your shirt, though.

STEVEN: You took off my shirt?

RUTHIE: No, you gave it to me.

STEVEN: (*Struggles up from couch.*) I'll be right back.

RUTHIE: Oh. Be careful. There's glass on the bathroom floor.

STEVEN: (*From offstage.*) How did glass get on the . . . Hey, there's somebody in here!

RUTHIE: Yeah, he was funny. You said he could stay.

STEVEN: (*From offstage.*) I said he could stay?

RUTHIE: You said any friend of Marty's was a bro of yours.

STEVEN: (*Trudging back on stage.*) I said that?

RUTHIE: Yeah. You didn't want him to get into another accident getting home.

STEVEN: Another accident?

RUTHIE: Well you accidentally hit him over his eyebrow with the ice tongs. But you stitched him up. You were awesome!

STEVEN: I stitched him up!?

RUTHIE: You're a doctor, right? You said, "No charge, bro!" You were awesome!

STEVEN: What did he do?

RUTHIE: Not much. He was out from the three Percocets you gave him.

STEVEN: I gave him drugs?

RUTHIE: You gave 'em out to everyone. Like Tic Tacs. But you couldn't have stitched him up otherwise. He was like a wild man

STEVEN: Look, I gotta call Leesa . . .

RUTHIE: That may not be so smart, after what you said.

STEVEN: What did I say?

RUTHIE: You really don't remember?

STEVEN: No.

RUTHIE: (*Smiling jovially.*) You stood up on that stool and shouted out to everyone that Leesa wore a size 31-A cup . . .

STEVEN: Oh, my God! I didn't!

RUTHIE: . . . and that she farted in her sleep. And you did the sound.

STEVEN: Oh, my God!

RUTHIE: That's when I realized who Leesa was.

STEVEN: How?

RUTHIE: You know that little cheese knife you put out on the cutting board?

STEVEN: What did she do?

RUTHIE: Well, she grabbed it and ran to your closet.

STEVEN: (*Races to his closet offstage.*) Oh, my God. She tore everything to ribbons!

RUTHIE: It was awesome actually.

STEVEN: (*Trudging back on stage.*) All my Jos. A. Bank's shirts. That bitch!

RUTHIE: Then she said she was going back to Iowa.

STEVEN: She said that?

RUTHIE: But that's not all.

STEVEN: No, that's gotta be all. I can't take anymore. I need something to drink.

RUTHIE: Yeah. About that . . .

STEVEN: Yeah?

RUTHIE: She emptied every bottle out in the toilet.

STEVEN: The eighteen-year old Glenlivet?

RUTHIE: (*Looking at watch.*) Yeah. But I could maybe run to the liquor store for you . . .

STEVEN: OK. I've got some money in my . . . what?

RUTHIE: (*Shaking her head.*) Um . . .

STEVEN: She took that too? My credit cards? My bank card?

RUTHIE: Yeah. But you didn't let it bother you.

STEVEN: I didn't?

RUTHIE: You said, you were gonna pull a Thoreau and go all Walden on her.

STEVEN: I said that?

RUTHIE: What does that mean, exactly?

STEVEN: (*Curling up now.*) Nothing. Nothing at all.

RUTHIE: Anyway, that's when the party began to break up a little bit.

STEVEN: Understandably.

RUTHIE: But there was still the couple with the bong . . .

STEVEN: The bong . . . ?

RUTHIE: Yeah. A few of us stayed and sang songs. She played a guitar. It was like the sixties.

STEVEN: Now I'm in my sixties . . .

RUTHIE: But he got angry when you asked her to play your skin flute.

STEVEN: Oh, I didn't.

RUTHIE: Yeah. Look, don't be too hard on yourself.

STEVEN: You didn't just say that.

RUTHIE: Because you said it jokingly. Anyone could see you weren't really serious. It was just a funny, awesome thing to say.

STEVEN: So, they left? The couple with the bong and the guitar?

RUTHIE: They would have. But you used those handcuffs to tie her to the radiator.

STEVEN: I don't have handcuffs.

RUTHIE: Well, someone did. When she started screaming you cut them off with an axe hidden in the closet. That's when the police came. Why would you need an axe in Manhattan?

STEVEN: The police came!?

RUTHIE: Yeah. They were very nice though.

STEVEN: The police were nice? Did they see the bong?

RUTHIE: Oh, no. That's what that glass was doing on the bathroom floor.

STEVEN: OK. Tell me

RUTHIE / STEVEN: You/I broke it with the axe.

STEVEN: I thought so. Then what did the police do?

RUTHIE: I told you, they were nice. They asked everyone to break it up. No pun intended. Then they took the axe as evidence.

STEVEN: Evidence of what?

RUTHIE: I don't remember. Attempted assault with a deadly weapon?

STEVEN: Oh, my God. And that's it, then?

RUTHIE: Pretty much.

STEVEN: Pretty much? What else? What else could possibly have happened last night?

RUTHIE: (*Smiling lasciviously.*) You were awesome.

STEVEN: Oh no.

RUTHIE: You were so gentle and yet wild at the same time. I can't remember the last time I had so many . . .

STEVEN: Ruthie! Ruthie, right? Stop! I'm sorry. I wasn't in my right mind.

RUTHIE: Oh, you were out of your mind, all right. Both of us were. I'll never forget it.

STEVEN: How long . . .

  (*RUTHIE puts her hands about eight inches apart.*)

STEVEN: Uh . . . I mean in time.

RUTHIE: Minutes . . . hours . . . days. Who knows? But you know what?

STEVEN: What?

RUTHIE: I love you too.

STEVEN: I said that? I said, "I love you?"

RUTHIE: Of course, you did, Silly.

STEVEN: But I never met you before.

RUTHIE: You said we were soul-mates and did I believe in love at first sight and you loved the way my eyes crinkled up at the corners when I laughed.

STEVEN: I used th . . . I said that?

RUTHIE: Yep. Now, how do you like your eggs, Doctor?

STEVEN: Ruthie . . . can I be honest with you?

RUTHIE: I hope so.

STEVEN: I'm not a doctor. I just played one on TV for seventeen years.

RUTHIE: But you did such a good job stitching that guy up.

STEVEN: I never even took Organic Chemistry.

RUTHIE: Well, I'm a little disappointed. But last night was . . . was . . . unforgettable. You were awesome!

STEVEN: Would you please stop saying that?!

RUTHIE: Saying what?

STEVEN: You were awesome! I wasn't awesome. I humiliated my fiancé and my brother, injured a guy I don't even know, offended a perfectly nice couple singing folk songs and broke their drug paraphernalia, and I may wind up a convicted felon for attempted murder and impersonating a doctor. That's not awesome. That's crazy.

RUTHIE: God, you are so awesome when you get inspired like that!

STEVEN: Look, you'd better go. I've gotta call the credit card companies. Where's my phone?

RUTHIE: (*Shrugs her shoulders.*) You want to use mine?

STEVEN: She took that too? You know what? I deserve it. I deserve it. I deserve to be punished for this.

RUTHIE: (*Holding up handcuffs.*) I agree, Huggy Buggy . . . .

STEVEN: What are you doing?

RUTHIE: (*Putting on handcuffs and attaching them to the bed.*) You've been a very bad boy. Ruthie's gonna spank the bad boy.

STEVEN: Look, I'm not in the mood. (*Pause.*) Ruthie?

RUTHIE: Yes, bad boy?

STEVEN: Close the bathroom door, OK? I don't want Scarface to wake up.

RUTHIE: Oh, good idea. Don't go anywhere. I'll be right back.

STEVEN: (*Looks directly at audience and tries to gesture "what-are-you-gonna-do?" while handcuffed to the bed.*) Awesome!

TEN-MINUTE PLAY PRODUCERS

The Actors Studio of Newburyport
TASN Short Play Festival
http://www.newburyportacting.org/
Contact Marc Clopton, info@newburyportacting.org

Acts on the Edge, Santa Monica
mariannesawchuk@hotmail.com

American Globe Theatre Turnip Festival,
Gloria Falzer
gfalzer@verizon.net

The Arc Theatre
arciTEXT Ten-Minute Play Festival
natalie@arctheatrechicago.org

Artistic Home Theatre Co.
Cut to the Chase Festival
Kathy Scambiatterra, Artistic Director: artistic.director@theartistichome.org

Artistic New Directions
Janice Goldberg, Co Artistic Director, ANDJanice@aol.com
Kristine Niven, Co Artistic Director, KNiven@aol.com
www.andtheatrecompany.org

Artist's Exchange
One Act Play Festival
Jessica Chace, Artistic Director, OAPF
jessica.chace@artists-exchange.org
www.artists-exchange.org

The ArtsCenter, Carrboro, NC
10x10 in the Triangle
Jeri Lynn Schulke, director
theatre@artscenterlive.org
www.artscenterlive.org

A-Squared Theatre Workshop
My Asian Mom Festival
Joe Yau (jyauza@hotmail.com)

Association for Theatre in Higher Education New Play Development Workshop
Contact Person: Charlene A. Donaghy
Email address of theatre/contact person: charlene@charleneadonaghy.com
Website of theatre: http://www.athe.org

Auburn Players Community Theatre Short Play Festival
Bourke Kemmedy
email: bourkekennedy@gmail.com
The Barn Theatre
www.thebarnplayers.org

Barrington Stage Company
10X10 New Play Festival
Julianne Boyd is the Artistic Director
jboyd@barringtonstageco.org
www.barringtonstageco.org

Belhaven University, Jackson, Mississippi
One Act Festival
Joseph Frost, Department Chair
theatre@belhaven.edu

Black Box Theatre
FIVES New Play Festival
Producer: Nancy Holaday
(719) 330-1798
nancy@blackboxdrama.com

Blue Slipper Theatre, Livingston, Montana
Marc Beaudin, Festival Director
blueslipper10fest@gmail.com
www.blueslipper.com

Boston Theatre Marathon
Boston Playwrights Theatre
www.bostonplaywrights.org
Kate Snodgrass (ksnodgra@bu.edu)
(Plays by New England playwrights only)

Boulder Life Festival, Boulder, Colorado
Dawn Bower, Director of Theatrical Program (dawn@boulderlifefestival.com)
www.boulderlifefestival.com

Box Factory for the Arts
Judith Sokolowski, President
boxfactory@sbcglobal.net
www.boxfactoryforthearts.org

The Brick's "Tiny Theater Festival"
Michael Gardner, Artistic Director
mgardner@bricktheater.com
www.bricktheater.com

Broken Nose Theatre
Benjamin Brownson, Artistic Director
Bechdel Fest
www.brokennosetheatre.com
ben@brokennosetheatre.com

The Brooklyn Generator
Erin Mallon
email: brooklyngenerator@outlook.com
website: https://www.thetanknyc.org/the-brooklyn-generator

Camino Real Playhouse
www.caminorealplayhouse.org

Chalk Repertory Theatre Flash Festival produced by Chalk Repertory Theatre
Contact person: Ruth McKee
ruthamckee@aol.com
www.chalkrep.com

Chameleon Theater Circle, Burnsville, MN 55306
www.chameleontheatre.org
jim@chameleontheatre.org

Chagrin Valley Little Theatre
10-10 New Plays Festival
www.cvlt.org
cvlt@cvlt.org

Changing Scene Theatre Northwest
ATTN: Pavlina Morris
changingscenenorthwest@hotmail.com

Cherry Picking
cherrypickingnyc@gmail.com

Chicago Indie Boots Festival
www.indieboots.org

City Theatre
www.citytheatre.com
Susan Westfall (susan@citytheatre.com)

City Theatre of Independence
Powerhouse Theatre
Annual Playwrights Festival
Powerhouse Theatre
www.citytheatreofindependence.org

The Collective New York
C10 Play Festival
www.thecollective-ny.org
thecollective9@gmail.com

Colonial Playhouse
Colonial Quickies
www.colonialplayhouse.net
colonialplayhousetheater@40yahoo.com

Company of Angels
P.O Box 3480. Los Angeles, CA 90078
Los Angeles, CA 90013
(213) 489-3703 (main office)
armevan@sbcglobal.net
https://www.companyofangels.org

Core Arts Ensemble
coreartsensemble@gmail.com

Därkhorse Drämatists
www.darkhorsedramatists.com
darkhorsedramatists@gmail.com

Distilled Theatre Co.
submissions.dtc@gmail.com

Edmonds Driftwood Players
www.driftwoodplayers.com
shortssubmissions@driftwoodplayers.com
tipsproductions@driftwoodplayers.com

Drilling Company
Hamilton Clancy
drillingcompany@aol.com

Durango Arts Center 10-Minute Play Festival
www.durangoarts.org
Theresa Carson
TenMinutePlayDirector@gmail.com

Eden Prairie Players
www.edenprairieplayers.com

Eastbound Theatre 10 minute Festival (in the summer: themed)
Contact Person: Tom Rushen
email: ZenRipple@yahoo.com

East Haddam Stage Company
Contact person: Kandie Carl
email: Kandie@ehsco.org

Emerging Artists Theatre
Fall EATFest
www.emergingartiststheatre.org

En Avant Playwrights
A community for playwrights to support and encourage each other to send out and produce their work.
https://www.tapatalk.com/groups/enavantplaywrights/

Ensemble Theatre of Chattanooga Short Attention Span Theatre Festival
Contact Person: Garry Posey (Artistic Director)
garryposey@gmail.com
www.ensembletheatreofchattanooga.com

Fell's Point Corner Theatre 10 x 10 Festival
Contact Person: Richard Dean Stover (rick@fpct.org)
www.fpct.org

Fem Noire (plays by New England women playwrights)
Image Theatre
Lowell, MA
www.imagetheater.com
imagetheaterlowell@gmail.com

Fine Arts Association
Annual One Act Festival-Hot from the Oven Smorgasbord
ahedger@fineartsassociation.org

Firehouse Center for the Arts, Newburyport, MA
New Works Festival
Kimm Wilkinson, Director
www.firehouse.org
Limited to New England playwrights

Flush Ink Productions
Asphalt Jungle Shorts Festival
http://www.flushink.net/flushink.html

The Fringe of Marin Festival
Contact Person: Annette Lust
email: jeanlust@aol.com

Fury Theatre
katie@furytheare.org
FUSHION: New Mexico's Professional Theatre Company
http://www.fusionabq.org
info@fusionabq.org

Future Ten
info@futuretenant.org

Gallery Players
Annual Black Box Festival
info@galleryplayers.com

Gaslight Theatre Company
www.gaslight-theatre.org
gaslighttheatre@gmail.com

GI60
Steve Ansell
screammedia@yahoo.com

The Gift Theater
TEN Festival
Contact: Michael Patrick Thornton
www.thegifttheatre.org

Good Acting Studio
Good Works Theatre Festival
www.goodactingstudio.com

The Greenhouse Ensemble
Ten-Minute Play Soiree
www.greenhouseensemble.com

Heartland Theatre Company
Themed 10-Minute Play Festival Every Year
Contact Person: Mike Dobbins (Artistic Director)
boxoffice@heartlandtheatre.org
www.heartlandtheatre.org

Hella Fresh Fish
freshfish2submit@gmail.com

Hobo Junction Productions
Hobo Robo Festival
Spenser Davis, Literary Manager
hobojunctionsubmissions@gmail.com
www.hobojunctionproductions.com

The Hovey Players, Waltham MA
Hovey Summer Shorts
www.hoveyplayers.com

Image Theatre
Naughty Shorts
jbisantz@comcast.net

Island Theatre 10-Minute Play Festival
www.islandtheatre.org

Ixion Ensemble, Lansing MI
Jeff Croff, Artistic Director
Ixionensemble@gmail.com

Kings Theatre
www.kingstheatre.ca

Lakeshore Players
https://www.lakeshoreplayers.org
Joan Elwell
office@lakeshoreplayers.org

Lee Street Theatre, Salisbury, NC (themed)
Original 10-Minute Play Festival
Justin Dionne, managing artistic director
info@leestreet.org
www.leestreet.org

Little Black Dress Ink
ATTN: Tiffany Antone
Email: info@LittleBlackDressINK.org
www.LittleBlackDressINK.org

Little Fish Theatre Co.
holly@littlefishtheatre.org
www.littlefishtheatre.org

Live Girls Theatre
submissions@lgtheater.org

Luna Stage
New Moon Short Play Festival
Email: lunatheater@gmail.com
www.lunastage.org

MadLab Theatre
Theatre Roulette
Andy Batt (andy@madlab.net)
www.madlab.net

Magnolia Arts Center, Greenville, NC
Ten Minute Play Contest
info@magnoliaartscenter.com
www.magnoliaartscenter.com
Fee charged

Manhattan Repertory Theatre, New York, NY
Ken Wolf
manhattanrep@yahoo.com
www.manhattanrep.com

McLean Drama Company
www.mcleandramacompany.org
Rachel Bail (rachbail@yahoo.com)

Miami 1-Acts Festival (two sessions—Winter (December) and Summer (July)
Contact: Steven A. Chambers, Literary Manager (schambers@new-theatre.org Ricky
J. Martinez, Artistic Director (rjmartinez@new-theatre.org)
Website of theatre: www.new-theatre.org
Submission Requirements No more than 10-15 pages in length; subject is not specific, though plays can reflect life in South Florida and the tropics and the rich culture therein. Area playwrights are encouraged to submit, though the festival is open to national participation. Deadline for the Winter Session is October 15 of each year; deadline for the Summer Session is May 1 of each year.

Milburn Stone Theatre One Act Festival
www.milburnstone.org

Mildred's Umbrella Theater Company
Museum of Dysfunction Festival
www.mildredsumbrella.com
e-mail: info@mildredsumbrella.com

Mill 6 Collaborative
John Edward O'Brien, Artistic Director
mill6theatre@gmail.com

Monkeyman Productions
The Simian Showcase
submissions@monkeymanproductions.com.
www.monkeymanproductions.com

Napa Valley Playhouse
8 x 10: A Festival of 10 Minute Plays
www.napavalleyplayhouse.org

Newburgh Free Academy
tsandler@necsd.net

The New American Theatre
www.newamericantheatre.com
Play Submissions: JoeBays44@earthlink.net

New Jersey Rep
Theatre Brut Festival
Their yearly Theatre Brut Festival is organized around a specified theme.
njrep@njrep.org

New Urban Theatre Laboratory
5 & Dime
Jackie Davis, Artistic Director
jackie.newurbantheatrelab@gmail.com

New Voices Original Short Play Festival
Kurtis Donnelly (kurtis@gvtheatre.org)

NFA New Play Festival
Newburgh Free Academy
201 Fullerton Ave, Newburgh, NY 12550
Terry Sandler (terrysandle@hotmail.com)
(may not accept electronic submissions)

North Park Playwright Festival
New short plays (no more than 15 pages, less is fine)
Submissions via mail to:
North Park Vaudeville and Candy Shoppe
2031 El Cajon Blvd.
San Diego, CA 92104
Attn: Summer Golden, Artistic Director.
www.northparkvaudeville.com

Northport One-Act Play Festival
Jo Ann Katz (joannkatz@gmail.com)
www.northportarts.org

The Now Collective
Sean McGrath
Sean@nowcollective@gmail.com

NYC Playwrights
Play of the Month Project
http://nycp.blogspot.com/p/play-of-month.html

Northwest 10 Festival of 10-Minute Plays
Sponsored by Oregon Contemporary Theatre
www.octheatre.org/nw10-festival
Email: NW10Festival@gmail.com

Onion Man Productions Summer Harvest
onionmanproductions@gmail.com

Open Tent Theatre Co.
Ourglass 24 Hour Play Festival
opententtheater@gmail.com

Otherworld Theatre
Paragon Festival—sci-fi and fantasy plays
Elliott Sowards, literary manager of Otherworld Theatre and curator of the Paragon
Play Festival, elliott@otherworldtheatre.org
https://www.otherworldtheatre.org/

Over Our Head Players, Racine WI
www.overourheadplayers.org/oohp15

Pandora Theatre, Houston, Texas
Vox Feminina
Melissa Mumper, Artistic Director
pandoratheatre@sbcglobal.net

Paw Paw Players One Act Festival
www.ppvp.org

Pegasus Theater Company (in Sonoma County, north of San Francisco)
Tapas Short Plays Festival
www.pegasustheater.com
Contact: Lois Pearlman lois5@sonic.net

Philadelphia Theatre Company
PTC@Play New Work Festival
Contact: Jill Harrison
Email: jillian.harrison@gmail.com
www.philadelphiatheatrecompany.org

PianoFight Productions, L.A.
ShortLivedLA@gmail.com

Piney Fork Press Theater Play Festival
Johnny Culver, submissions@pineyforkpress.com
www.pineyforkpress.com

The Playgroup, LLC
Boca Raton, FL
Email: theplaygroupllc@gmail.com
www.theplaygroupllc.com

Playhouse Creatures
Page to Stage
newplays@playhousecreatures.org

Play on Words Productions
playonwordsproductions@gmail.com
Megan Kosmoski, Producing Artist Director

Playmakers Spokane
Hit & Run
Sandra Hosking
playmakersspokane@gmail.com

Playpalooza
Backstage at SPTC (Santa Paula Theatre Co.)
John McKinley, Artistic Director
sptcbackstage@gmail.com

Playwrights' Arena
Flash Theater LA
Contact person: Jon Lawrence Rivera
email: jonlawrencerivera@gmail.com
www.playwrightsarena.org

Playwrights' Round Table, Orlando, FL
Summer Shorts
Chuck Dent charlesrdent@hotmail.com
www.theprt.com

Playwrights Studio Theater
5210 W. Wisconsin Ave.
Milwaukee, WI 53208
Attn: Michael Neville, Artistic Dir.

Renegade Theatre Festival
www.renegadetheatrefestival.org/

Salem Theatre Co.
Moments of Play
New England playwrights only
mop@salemtheatre.com

Santa Cruz Actors Theatre
Eight Tens at Eight
Wilma Chandler, Artistic Director
ronziob@email.com
http://www.sccat.org

Secret Room Theatre
Contact: Alex Dremann
Email: alexdremann@me.com
www.secretroomtheatre.com

Secret Rose Theatre
www.secretrose.com
info@secretrose.com

Secret Theatre (Midsummer Night Festival), Queens, NY
Odalis Hernandez, odalis.hernandez@gmail.com
www.secrettheatre.com/

She Speaks, Kitchener, Ontario
Paddy Gillard-Bentley (paddy@skyedragon.com)
Women playwrights

Shelterbelt Theatre, Omaha, NB
From Shelterbelt with Love
McClain Smouse, associate-artistic@shelterbelt.org
submissions@shelterbelt.org
www.shelterbelt.org

Shepparton Theatre Arts Group
"Ten in 10" is a performance of ten plays each running for ten minutes every year.
Email: info@stagtheatre.com
www.stagtheatre.com

Short+Sweet
Literary Manager, Pete Malicki
Pete@shortandsweet.org
http://www.shortandsweet.org/shortsweet-theatre/submit-script

Silver Spring Stage, Silver Spring, MD
Jacy D'Aiutolo
oneacts2012.ssstage@gmail.com
www.ssstage.org

Sixth Street Theatre
Snowdance 10-Minute Comedy Festival
Rich Smith
Snowdance318@gmail.com

Source Festival
jenny@culturaldc.org

Southern Repertory Theatre
6 x 6
Aimee Hayes (literary@southernrep.com)
www.southernrep.com/

Stage Door Productions
Original One-Act Play Festival
www.stagedoorproductions.org

Stage Door Repertory Theatre
www.stagedoorrep.org

Stage Q
www.stageq.com

Stillwater Short Play Festival
Town and Gown Theatre (Stillwater, OK)
Debbie Sutton (producer)
snobiz123@aol.com

Stonington Players
HVPanciera@aol.com

Stratton Summer Shorts
Stratton Players
President: Rachel D'onfro
www.strattonplayers.com
info@strattonplayers.com

Subversive Theatre Collective
Kurt Schneiderman, Artistic Director
www.subversivetheatre.org
info@subversivetheatre.org

Ten Tuckey Festival
doug@thebardstown.com

The Theatre Lab
733 8th St., NW
Washington, DC 20001
https://www.theatrelab.org/
Contact: Buzz Mauro (buzz@theatrelab.org, 202-824-0449)

Theatre Odyssey
Sarasota, Florida
Tom Aposporos Vice President
www.theatreodyssey.org

Theatre One Productions
theatreoneproductions@yahoo.com

Theatre Out, Santa Ana CA
David Carnevale david@theatreout.com
LGBT plays

Theatre Oxford 10 Minute Play Contest
http://www.theatreoxford.com
Alice Walker
10minuteplays@gmail.com

Theatre Roulette Play Festival
Madlab Theatre Co.
andyb@mablab.net

Theatre Three
www.theatrethree.com
Jeffrey Sanzel (jeffrey@theatrethree.com)

Theatre Westminster
Ten Minute New (And Nearly New) Play Festival
ATTN: Terry Dana Jachimiak II
jachimtd@westminster.edu

Theatre Works 10-Minute Play Festival
https://theatreworks.us/playfestival-event.php

Those Women Productions
www.thosewomenproductions.com

TouchMe Philly Productions
www.touchmephilly.wordpress.com
touchmephilly@gmail.com

Towne Street Theatre Ten-Minute Play Festival
info@townestreet.org

Underground Railway Theatre
https://www.centralsquaretheater.org/about/underground-railway-theater/
Debra Wise, Artistic Director (debra@undergroundrailwaytheatre.org)

Unrenovated Play Festival
unrenovatedplayfest@gmail.com

Walking Fish Theatre
freshfish2submit@gmail.com

Weathervane Playhouse
8 X 10 Theatrefest
info@weathervaneplayhouse.com

Wide Eyed Productions
www.wideeyedproductions.com
playsubmissions@wideeyedproductions.com

Winston-Salem Writers
Annual 10 Minute Play Contest
www.wswriters.org
info@wswriters.org

Write Act
www.writeactrep.org
John Lant (j316tlc@pacbell.net)